# A STROLL IN JAINISM

## (Upādhyāya Amar Muni Commemoration Volume)

Editors
Ram Mohan Das
Neeraj Kumar

**Kaveri Books**
New Delhi - 110 002

Title: A Stroll in Jainism: (Upādhyāya Amar Muni Commemoration Volume)
Editors: Ram Mohan Das and Neeraj Kumar



First Published 2002
Edition 2025

ISBN-10: 81-7479-048-9
ISBN-13: 978-81-7479-048-4

Price: Rs. 750.00



*Published by*
**Kaveri Books**
4832/24, Ansari Road
New Delhi-110002 (India)
Tel: 011- 47072321
E-mail : info@kaveribooks.com
kaveribooks@gmail.com
Website: www.kaveribooks.com

**PRINTED IN INDIA**

*Upādhyāya Amar Muni : Soul of Jainism*

LOTUS IN WATER

प्राणानामनिलेन वृत्तिरुचिता सत्कल्पवृक्षे वने
तोये काञ्चन पद्मरेणुकपिशे धर्माभिषेकक्रिया।
ध्यानं रत्नशिलातलेषु विबुधस्त्रीसन्निधौ संयमः।
यद् वाञ्छन्ति तपोभिरन्य मुनयः तस्मिन्तपस्यन्त्यमी॥

# श्रीअमराष्टकम्

अराग: अद्वेष: अकोप: अचिन्त:,
अरोग: अभोग: अदीन: अहीन:।
सदा नि:स्पृहो भावलीन: समाधौ,
जितक्षोभमायाममत्वादिदोष:॥ 1 ॥

प्रशान्त: प्रबुद्ध: सदात्मानुरागी,
अनासक्तयोगी वियोगिस्वबन्धु:।
जराजन्मदावानलवारिवाह:
करे दंडधारी दयापूर्णचित्त:॥ 2 ॥

निरीह: अमानी गुणागाररूप:,
जगत्पारकर्त्ता महन्नाविकोऽसौ।
प्रसन्नानन: सर्वनाथ: प्रकृष्ट:
सदा सज्जनानन्ददाता दयालु:॥ 3 ॥

निरातंकवृत्ति: सदानन्दभोक्ता,
प्रगल्भ: पुनीत: अहंभावहीन:।
स्वयं लब्धमुक्ति: नराणां च नेता,
जगत्कालकूटात् च त्राता महेश:॥ 4 ॥

न विरक्ति: न रत्नेऽनुरक्ति:,
न रंके घृणा नापि राज्ञि प्रसक्ति:।
मदीयं त्वदीयं न कश्चिद् विचार:,
सदा साम्ययोगी सदैवैकदर्शी॥ 5॥

न वस्त्राभिलाषी न चाकाशवासी:
स्वयं मध्यमार्गी विचारे प्रचारे।
उदार: वदान्य: सदा तत्त्वद्रष्टा,
हितैषी परार्थानुचिन्तानिमग्न:॥ 6॥

न धर्मे न चार्थे न कामे न मोक्षे,
न लोकैषणथां मदीया प्रवृत्ति:।
इयं मेऽभिलाषां भवत्पादमूले
अनन्यानुराग: भवेद् बद्धमूल:॥ 7 ॥

त्वदीया सुकीर्त्तिः दिशः पूरयित्वा,
प्रयाता दिवं गीयमानाऽप्सरोभिः।
शरीरे विनष्टे यशःकायरूपे,
जरामृत्युभीत्या विमुक्तः स्थितोऽसि॥ 8॥

अमराष्टकमिदं पुण्यं, सर्वपापप्रमोचकम्।
यः पठेत् पाठयेत् गायेत् स लभते परमं पदम्॥

—**Editors**

## Dedication

Milky Silky rosy face
Tender slender bodily grace
O My Mother Divine
Thou be mine
I be Thine
So do I pine

कुपुत्रो जायेत क्वचिदपि कुमाता न भवति

—Editors

# Preface

Jainism has been acknowledged as a great religion of the world. It is not only a religion but also spiritual philosophy capable of enlightening human life both internally as well as externally. It is imbued both in Indian thought and Indian culture alike. In Indian culture, *Guru* has got an important place. He has been, in fact, given higher place than the Almighty. It is the *Guru* who guides the way to God. God resides in the heart of those who give due respect to *Guru*. A man cannot attain 'Knowledge' without being blessed by *Guru*. Even the Devās, Asurās, and Kings have been blessed by *Guru*. Āchārya Brithaspati was the *Guru* of the Devās, *Guru* Śukrachārya of the Asurās, Brahmarśi, Vasistha of the great Suryavanśi Kings and Maharśi Śandilya of the Yādavas. Dronachārya was the *Guru* of the Kauravas and the Pāndavas. The great philosopher Socrates was the *Guru* of Alexander, the Great. Sri Rāmakrishna Paramhamsa was the *Guru* of Swami Vivekānanda. Sikhism is totally based on the tradition of ten *Gurus*. The first *Guru* was Sri Nānak Dev and the last was Sri Govind Singh Ji. In Buddhism also, there has been a continuous tradition of the *Gurus* in the form of Bodhisattvas starting from Lord Buddha. Jainism is also based on the tradition of twenty four Tirthankaras. In Jain religion, the *Gurus* have been adorned with the titles of 'Āchārya' and 'Upādhyāya'.

Upādhyāya Amar Muni has rightly observed, "In the terms of meditation, that guide is *Guru* whose life has been enlightened by celestial qualities and who wishes to take the people on the same enlightened path". "Swami Vivekānanda has also said, "The teacher, like a gardener, helps the student manifest his innate divinity. The teacher must know that he is not giving something new to the student but only is helping him bring out what is latent in him."

The title of *Guru* or *Gurudeva* has been conferred on the great persons. Kavindra Rabindra Nath Tagore was called 'Gurudeva' by Mahatma Gandhi. Mahākavi Kālidāsa has been called 'Kavi kula Guru'. The great saint Amar Muni Ji Mahārāja has been adorned with the titile of 'Gurudeva'.

Upādhyāya Amar Muni, a sharp metaphysicist was a profound thinker, an eminent scholar and a saint of the highest order. He was born on the auspicious day of Śarat Purnima in 1903 in Godha, a small village rich in naturel surroundings and situated in Nārnaul, a hilly town in present Haryaṇa. His father's name was Lal Singh and mother's name was Chameli Devi. He was initiated in the monastic order at the tender age of eleven. He possessed keen intellect, so he mastered himself not only in Jain scriptures but also in Vedic and Buddhistic ones. He made their comparative study and deeply thought over them and understood and interpreted them in rightful way. His conviction was that detachment, selfless service and knowing oneself are the essence of all the religions.

He was known all over India for his progressive interpretation of Jain scriptures in consonance with the present day scientific creative revolution. He vehemently attacked the evils lying in social, religious ana political life of the people and offered practical solution to meet and solve them.

He had to his credit a great number of publications in almost all the forms of literary composition and in most of the problems of human behaviour both in individual as well as social context. He was the first Jain ascetic who thought deeply on both the problems of this as well as the other world. He laid great emphasis on the coordination of man and society. Being a rare combination of man and superman, he devoted his entire life equally for the cause of religion and humanity.

He was a devoted votary of *Anekāntavāda*. So his line of thinking was truth oriented and free from prejudices and thus scientific and based on rightful thinking. He held that virture and vice do not lie in action but in intention.

Munishree was a true patriot. When Mahatma Gandhi was at Noakhali trying his level best to extinguish the blazing fire of communal hatred between the Hindus and the Muslims and to establish harmony and goodwill between them, he went there and met Mahatmaji and as a true follower of non-violence offered his services there. Not only this much, he also took keen active interest in political matters also. Whenever he saw that there was tension among the leaders of different political parties, he personally went to them and by his political insight and logical arguments he very often succeeded in removing the differences and bring about compromise. It was in appreciation of his patriotism that Smt. Indira Gandhi, the then Prime Minister of India, decorated him with the tilte of *Rāstrasant.*

Munishree, a true karmayogi, firmly believed in the truth of the adage, 'It behoves the great to be always active : on the pretext of being an ascetic who had renounced the world and severed all his connections with it, he never kept himself aloof from the world and its problems. He participated heart and soul in all the affairs and tried to lead the people on the righteous path'.

In the year 1962 during his *chaturmās* in Rājgir while meditating in the *Saptaparni* cave of *Vaibhāragiri* he conceived the idea of Veerāyatan in this wonderful site hollowed with its historical and spiritual background. In 1972, at the time of the 2500$^{th}$ *Nirvāna* centenary of Lord Mahāveer he placed before an audience of monks, scholars and intellectuals the concept of Veerāyatan. In 1973, his dream received a concrete form. Despite strong and sustained opposition from the local illiterate and backward people, Munishree succeeded in laying the foundation of Veerāyatan in the sylvan surrounding just at the foot of the *Vaibhāragiri.* Under his affectionate patronage it soon rose into prominence as a premier Jain spiritual institution. Now it has its branches in countries like U.K, U.S.A. Canada and Africa.

Munishree had great respect for others' sentiments. Whenever a devotee came to him and offered a present, he, though himself totally free from desire, accepted it, thinking that his refusal might hurt his feelings. But as soon as the donor left the place, he handed it over to the person who was in need of it.

He thought deeply of the different deformities of the society and offered a practical solution to those problems. Accordingly, he called for a creative revolution in the society of woman and attacked vehemently the differences between the man and the woman. In ancient India, woman was given the status of a goddess. It was the ancient Indian culture about which he says, "The country in which woman was once worshipped like a god now looks down upon her. It is not religion. It is non religion".

Pt. Jawaharlal Nehru, the first Prime Minister of India, throwing light on the importance of woman has said, "For awakening the public, we have to awaken the woman first. When she will march on the path of progress, the family will progress, the village will move, the town will move, the nation will progress". Even Smt. India Gandhi has said, "The country in which the woman has progressed has achieved the highest position in the world. And the country in which the woman was inactive, insulted and downtrodden, lagged behind."

Upādhyāya Shree was a great champion of the cause of women. So he supported the importance as described in the ancient Vedas, Upanishadas, Jain Literature and Tripitakas. He has sung the glory of woman in the times of the Rāmāyana and the Mahābhārata. He presents the sublime form of Sita, Draupadi, Kunti etc. in strongest possible words. Describing the divine qualities of a few women of the time of Shraman Bhagwān Mahāveer, he says, "The venerable woman of the age of Mahāveer Bhagwān such Ārya Chandanā, Mrigawati Jayanti etc. are shining stars of our history. The life of Ārya Chandanā is the pious Triveni of Karma, Knowledge and power which will keep on flowing as a source of inspiration for all human beings for all the time to come. The story of suffering of Chandankalā is the burning example of the devilish nature and social disorder of the then male-dominated society. Mahāveer brought her out of the suffering life who was the unextinguishable light of 'Karma Yoga' and made her the chief spokeswoman of a huge 'Sangha' of 36000 sādhavis whom she led very successfully. On 26th January, 1987, he bestowed upon her the title of Āchārya. Mahāraj Amarmuni has mentioned the luminous ladies of the Buddhist Tripitakas' and Jātak stories whose lives are ideals for the whole of womenfolk. This great saint Upādhyāya Shree Amarmuni left for his heavenly abode on June 1, 1992 at 4.30 p.m. Really, he was a great philosopher, social worker and preacher. He was the symbol of humanity, peace, simplicity and equality.

The papers in this volume deal with various facets of Jainism. They highlight the growing academic interest of scholars in the field of Jainological studies and research.

We shall consider ourselves fully rewarded if the present work awakens new interest in the study of Jainism. We are deeply indebted to all those who are pioneers in the field of Jainological studies.

We take this opportunity to convey our humble and sincere thanks to all contributors who immediately responded to our request and contributed their learned papers to this volume, making it a success.

In the end our thanks go to Rakesh Goel, proprietor, Kaveri Books, New Delhi with whose good will and active co-operation the present volume could be published in such a short time.

The editors earnestly solicit constructive criticism from careful and conscientious readers.

**Ram Mohan Das**

**Neeraj Kumar**

# Contributors


1. L. M. Singhvi, M.P.
   Senior Advocate,
   Supreme Court of India
   President, IGNCA
   New Delhi.

2. D. C. Jain
   Professor & Head
   P. G. Centre of Commerce & Applied Economics
   H.D. Jain College, Ara (Bihar)

3. K. P. Krishna
   Professor & Head
   P. G. Centre of Psychology
   Gaya College, Gaya (Bihar)

4. M. K. Sharan
   Professor & Head
   P. G. Centre of A. I. & A. S.
   Gaya College, Gaya (Bihar)

5. V. R. Agrawal
   Professor, P. G. Centre of Sanskrit Gaya College,
   Gaya (Bihar)

6. P. C. Jain
   (Retd.) Principal
   D.H.S.K. Commerce College,
   Dibrugarh (Assam)

7. P. Chenna Reddy
   Head, School of History, Culture & Archaeology
   P. S. Telugu University
   Srisailam (A.P.)

8. D. C. Jain
   Secretary, Research Foundation for Jainology
   Chennai (Tamil Nadu)

9. C. M. Agrawal
   Reader in History
   Kumaun University,
   Almora (Uttaranchal)

10. M.P. Chaurasia
    Reader in Philosophy
    Jai Prakash University,
    Chhapra (Bihar)

11. Neeraj Kumar
    Lecturer in English
    Magadh University,
    Bodh Gaya (Bihar)

12. Vimal Bafanā
    Research Scholar
    University of Pune,
    Pune (Maharashtra)

# Contents

# Jainism : An Overview

1

*Upādhyāya Amar Muni*

When a man tinged in the colour of sectarianism starts supporting his own doctrines and refuting those of others, then he sometimes adopts highly dangerous means. Difference of opinion in respect of any matter is not so bad as filling in it the poison of hatred. In India the sectarian differences have become so terrible, bitter and poisonous that even our indivisible nationalism is on the point of being shattered.

The Hindus call the Muslims as *mlechha* and the Muslims call the Hindus as *kāfir.* Similarly some people call Jains as atheists. This means that whatsoever comes in the mind of man he calls other sects in that way. He does not give the least thought to the fact that what he says is true or not and what would be its result. To impose false allegation on anybody and spread hatred against him, is not only improper but highly immoral.

## Jainism is Theistic

Jainism is absolutely theistic. To call it atheistic is quite illogical. Why the people of India started calling Jainism as atheistic has a history behind it. When because of ignorance the performance of sacrifices etc. was propagated and in the name of religion the killing of the poor and dumb animals had come into vogue, then Lord Mahāveer vehemently opposed this violence based on superstition. The basic and main works that supported sacrifices etc. were the *Vedas.* As they supported violence so they were regarded by Lord Mahāveer as unauthoritative. This led to great agitation among the followers of the Vedic cult. They got mentally irritated. But they could not meet the conclusive logic given by Jainism. They only raised noise that those who do not believe in the *Vedas* and censure them are atheists. Since then uptodate this false allegation is being imposed on Jainism. Not meeting logic with logic and start abusing is evidently nothing but prejudice and sectarian bias. Any neutral thinker can say that this is not the criterion of deciding about the truth.

If the followers of the Vedic religion call Jainism atheistic on the ground that it calumniates the *Vedas* then the Jains also may call the Vedic religion as atheistic as it calumniates Jainism. But this is not the right way. It is not reasonable to say that who does not believe in Vedic works is an atheist and who does not believe in Jainism is not an atheist. But the truth is that none can be called an atheist only on the ground that he does not believe in the religious works of the other religion. Were it so then all the religious would have become atheist because it is obvious that all of them in respect of their religious rites are here and there against one another. It is regrettable that even in the present progressive age such baseless logic is applied and unnecessarily murdering the truth, one calls the other an atheist.

Jainism has no malice against the *Vedas.* It does not oppose them because of any sense of malice. How can Jainism, the supporter of equality censure any religion? It is ready to accept with all humility the truth propounded even by its greatest rival. It does not oppose the *Vedas* as a whole but only their such portions as prescribe goat-sacrifice, horse-sacrifice etc, which are full of violence. It openly opposes violence so it can never tolerate such cruel murder of animals committed in the name of religion.

In favour of calling Jainism as atheistic now a days one more reason is given but is also totally baseless. They say that "as Jainism does not believe in Supreme Soul, so it is atheistic".

Jainism does believe in Supreme Soul, but it has its own definite views about it. In its opinion the Supreme Soul is absolutely free from passion, malice and birth and death, has attained *Kevalajñāna* and *Kevaladarśana,* has neither body nor sense-organs nor actions nor gets their fruit and is free from old age, is immortal *siddha,* enlightened and pure soul. Jainism believes only in such passionless Supreme Soul. It sees in every soul this very Supreme light hidden in it and says that every *sādhaka* can by worshipping such passionless souls attain the position of the Supreme Soul. Then can we say that Jainism does not believe in Supreme Soul ?

The followers of Vedic religion may say that Jainism does not believe in such a form of Supreme Soul as we do and so it is atheistic. It is not a valid logic but *sectarian bias.* Even they whom they call atheists are not unanimous in respect of the form of the Supreme Soul. Muslims have different form of their God and Christians different one. Even in Vedic religion the God of *Sanātana Dharma* is different from the God of *Āryasamāja.* According to the former God can incarnate himself but God of Āryasamāja cannot do so. Then how can we say which is theistic and which is atheistic ? If only by believing in Supreme Soul any religion is theistic then Jainism also, according to its definition, believes in Supreme Soul and so it also is theistic.

Some scholars even say that as the Jainism does not accept God as the creator of the world, so it is atheistic. This logic also is baseless. If God is free from passion and malice will he create such a world as is full of dreadful mental agonics and physical ailments ? How can freedom from passion and malice be possible in the creator of such a world ? And without body creation itself is not possible. Thus in the Supreme Soul there exists no attribute of creatorship of this world.

A thing can be accepted only when it exists. Man has no wings. If any one comes and asks you to accept that man has wings, otherwise you are an atheistic. This will be nothing but choking the throat of the truth.

In Vedic tradition also such philosophies as Mīmāṁsā, Sānkhya and Vaiśeṣika etc. do not believe in God. They do not accept even His existence. So there the question of his being the creator of the world does not arise at all. But even they are called theistic and the Jainism which accepts the existence of the Supreme Soul is treated atheistic. It is nothing but false attachment for one's belief and baseless malice against that of others. In the present age of intellectualism such thinking has no importance.

Grammar decides the real meaning of words. So in this respect scholars regard only grammar as authority. Words theism and atheism belong to Sanskrit. So we shall determine their meaning on the basis of Pāṇini's grammar which belongs to the Vedic tradition.

While commenting on the aphorism of Pāṇini (*Aṣṭādhyāyī* 4.4.60) Bhattoji Dixit in his *Siddhānta Kaumudī* says, "one, who believes in the next world, is a theist and one who does not, is an atheist."

Any-right-thinking person can well see what the grammar says about these two words and what some of our friends say, Jainism accepts the soul and also the Supreme Soul and has faith in the endless power of the soul. It accepts the right of every soul to become the Supreme Soul. It accepts the next world rebirth, sin and virtue, the world and liberation, then who can dare call it atheistic. That faith cannot be atheistic in which at every step the Ganga of non-violence and compassion is flowing in which giving up every thing for the truth, good conduct, and the difficult path of *sādhanā* are accepted and in which immortal note of auspicious words of great men like passionless Lord Mahāveer is reverberating. Even then if Jainism is called atheistic then not a single religion of the world can be called theistic.

## God is not the creator of the world

Religions like Vedic, Islam and Christianity etc, regard God as the creator and protector of this world. Though there exist sufficient mutual differences in respect of the process of the creation of the world, yet on the question of accepting God as the creator of the world, they all are unanimous.

But the path of Jainism is quite different. It regards the world as eternal and endless. It holds that this world was neither ever created nor will ever be destroyed. Only the form of the matter changes, the matter itself is never destroyed. Only the form of the world changes. Land comes into existence in the place of a sea and sea in the place of land. Totally deserted regions become populated and populated ones deserted and lonely. Part annihilation has been taking place but it is not at all possible that one day there will be complete annihilation and every thing will be destroyed and the world will have to be created a new.

Yet many of our neighbouring religions accept the creation of the world. They are unable to believe that a thing can exist without being created. So they say, "The world is created by God". On this point Jain philosophy asks : "Can a thing not exist without being created ? If not, then how does God exist ? Who has created Him?" None created God and yet He exists since eternity. Similarly the world also for its existence needs no creator. It also like God is self-existent.

All accept that God is formless. He possesses neither body nor hands nor feet. Jainism argues : How can God who has no body, no hands and no feet, create this world ? We see that a potter and a goldsmith prepare things only with the help of their hands etc. No person having no body, can create any thing.

Muslims say that Khudā by His order created the world. He uttered *'Kuna'* and the world was created. We ask, "Has Khudā body ? Has He mouth ?" Muslims say, "Khudā has no limbs like body, mouth, tongue etc. We are surprised as to when Khudā has neither mouth nor tongue then how could he utter *'Kuna'*. For uttering a word mouth is essential. Further, the molecules themselves, which change into the form of the world are inert-without ears. How could they hear the order of Khudā ? If Khudā can speak, then why does he not speak now ? Today people get crazy in course of offering prayers to Khudā and even then he does not speak. If he starts speaking even today thousands of *Kāfirs* may turn Muslims. What a noble act of merit and benevolence it will be. Does Khudā not like all this ?

The *Sanātanist* as well as the *Āryasamājist* who follow the Vedic religion hold that God, at his sweet will creates this World.

As soon as God desires that the world be created, the earth, the sky, the sun, the moon, the rivers and the seas etc. come into existence.

Against this also Jain philosophy argues : "When God possesses no mind, then how can He desire ? Even desire has some purpose behind it, what is the purpose of God behind creating this world. God is kind, Supreme Father. How can He desire to create such a world as is full of wicked and carnivorous creatures like lions and serpents, is surrounded by diseases, sorrows, ill-will and evil habits and is pervaded with crimes such as theft, infidelity, robbery and murder." You will say, "This is the sport of God." What type of sport is this ? The poor worldly being suffer from awful distresses like diseases and sorrows and at the time of famine and flood hell-like lamentation is produced all over and you say all this the sport of God. There is not a single good man who will be willing to witness this sport. Had kind God created this world He would not have created the poor and miserable beings looking at whom our heart wells up with pity. While creating and then putting them in such a plight, if God feels no pity then how can we call Him kind ?

Older *Sanātanists* say that when the sinner and the wicked multiply in the world, then to destroy them God descends on the earth. *Āryasamājists* also hold that though God does not descend yet He definitely punishes the wicked. Jainism says, "God is Omniscent. He knows from before that such and such persons will become sinners and wicked and harass his creation. Then why does He create them ? It is not wise first to plant a poison tree and afterwards to cut it down. No sensible person will first spoil the clothes in mud and then wash them".

The second thing in this connection is: Are the sinners stronger than God himself ? Can God not prevent them from committing crime ? God who can at His mere will create such a gigantic world, can He not make his libertine subjects virtuous ? Had He possessed even a little pity. He must have certainly utilized His power to make the wicked good. Is it justified not to check the criminals while they commit sin and afterwards punish and destroy them ? Why did the Almighty first allow to grow in them the sense of committing crime ? You will say that God has granted freedom to living beings to act as they like, so He cannot prevent them. Think over it, is it the real freedom ? Freedom is granted for doing good action, not for doing bad ones. Will any just and subject-loving ruler do so ? First let his subjects commit theft and crime and then punish them for that. In the present progressive era such a foolish ruler cannot remain on the throne even for a single day.

If God is absolutely free from passion and malice then why does He take the trouble of creating this world ? Such a God can never like to get involved in the game of creating and destroying the world. As in doing so He shall have always to face passion and malice, make one happy and the other sorry, one rich and the other poor and provide one with Kaśmir-like beautiful place to live in and the other a scorching desert. Without the existence of passion and malice such a discriminatory attitude is not possible.

If one says that God does not do so at his own will then we may ask under whose direction He does so. If He performs such inauspicious actions at the direction of others then such a dependent agency can never be God. Then the force directing him to work shall be the real God. Secondly, God has fulfilled all his duties, has left nothing to perform. If He performs wordly duties then He cannot remain so, and like the wordly beings He too, will become an ordinary person entangled in the world.

At this point people may raise the same old logic, God does not act himself, He only grants men the fruit of their actions. This logic may satisfy a dull man but if one applies one's wisdom its hollowness automatically becomes apparent. With the help of a beautiful example this point may be answered.

There is a rich man. He has performed an evil action, the fruit of which he can get only by means of his wealth being stolen. God himself does not come to steal his wealth. He gets it stolen by a thief. In this context if a thief steals his wealth what would be the result. Any right thinking man may say that here the rich man gets the fruit of his previous action and the thief commits a guilt afresh. God gives the thief the fruit of his action. The judge sends him to the jail. Now say whether the thief stole the wealth at his own initiative or on motivation from God. If he did so on his own accord, then the rich man got the fruit of his action automatically, not from God. If the thief stole the wealth at the motivation from God, then he was innocent. Then on what ground God caused the judge to award punishment to the thief ? First causing the thief to steal and then getting him punished is no justice at all.

It is an example. By it alone the controversy is settled. If we accept that God involves himself in all the worldly affairs and grants the fruit of action then He himself shall be held responsible for all the atrocities and crimes committed in the world. Thus behind all the fruits of actions that we get, there is the hand of God. Thus it is an interesting spectacle; God is guilty and the living beings suffer punishment. Jainism does not regard God as the creator of the world and giver of the fruit of action. At this point many of our friends say, "If God cannot free us from sorrow and grant happiness, then what is the utility of devotion to him ? Devotion to such a God as does no good to us, is quite an useless. Jainism gives the answer. Does devotion simply mean; getting our work done; can there be no devotion to God without making Him the doer of action? It is no devotion but a kind of business. The devotion of those who treat God as the doer of action, is no devotion at all. It is simply trying to cajole, to flatter and to bribe God for our own happiness." According to Jainism only desireless devotion to God is the true and superb devotion. Now arises a question whether such a devotion is of any advantage to us or not ? The answer to it is : God is the highest ideal of spiritual excellence and it is only through devotion that he can be properly recognised. It is the principle of psychology that if a man continuously thinks about a thing he, in due course, adopts that very form and attitude as one wishes, so one becomes. According to this rule by thinking, reflecting and praying God one can attain the state of Supreme Soul. Is it an insignificant gain ?

One thing more. It has already been said earlier that Jainism has full faith in the existence of God and as such offers prayers and devotion to Him, not as the giver of happiness and sorrow but on account of His great and ideal qualities.

It accepts God in the form of a highly purified soul and places as an ideal, this very spiritual piety before every *Sādhaka.*

**Theory of Ascent**

Brahmanism believes in the theory of descent. It holds that God is the supreme power. He descends on the earth adopting the forms of man etc. and destroys unrighteousness and establishes righteousness. This is the fundamental idea of the theory of descent. Brahmanism holds that all the great men such as Ram and Krishna etc. who existed in the world, are the incarnations of God who with a view to removing the burden of the earth, are born from time to time, adopting different forms.

As against this *Śramaṇa* cultures, may it be Jain or Buddhist, has no faith whatsoever in the theory of descent. From the very beginning the ideal of *Śramaṇa* culture has been that there is neither God nor any other Supreme Power which creates and destroys this world. So when there exists no folk-fabricated omnipotent God Himself, then there is no question of His descent. Even if there be any ominscent and Omnipotent God, why should He come down on the earth and adopt the forms of fish, boar and men etc ? Can He not by his endless strength, remove the burden of the earth, from the very place where He resides ?

At the root of the theory of descent works the sense of inferiority of the human mind. It means that man is after all mere man. How can he perform such great feats ? So all the universally beneficent great men in this world were actually not men but were basically incarnations of God. As they were God so they performed such great and marvellous feats. How could a helpless man perform such feats ?

The theory of descent propounds inferiority of man, treats him as crippled, helpless and destitute. Whenever there is an occasion for performing a great work and shattering the cloud of calamity and atrocity, surrounding the country and the religion, then it recommends to wait for the incarnation of God; with pitiable and lowly mental attitude to sit at His feet implore him to descent at the earlist as He alone is the destroyer of our distress and only He can bring about the desired change.

The theory of descent asks man not to do any thing at his own initiative; as he is a man, merely a stupid man he cannot do any thing. How can a lowly man, having only a pair of hands and skeleton of bones and flesh, perform the work of God ? To vie with God is atheism, foolishness of the highest order. Thus the theory of descent is basically the flag-bearer of savish mentality.

A culture based on the theory of descent, has no faith in the superiority and purity of man. It tacitly accepts that man is nothing except a biped; his own future is not in his hand, but lies in the hands of the Almighty who can do what He likes; man is a puppet in His hands. In the words of the *Purāṇas,* God is totally free to do, to undo or to do otherwise; He is the Supreme Sovereign of the universe. As a potter revolves the lump of clay on his wheel, so God also by the power of *māyā* revolves the whole world (Gītā 18.61). In spite of his highest *Sādhanā* and attainment of the highest peaks of truth and non-violence, a man can never become God. There is a limit to man's development and that limit is determined by and is subordinate to God's wish. So a man should ever beg for God's grace. This is why God of the cultures other than *Śramaṇa* culture says, "O man! take shelter with me and remember me. Why do you fear ? I shall free you from all sins. Do not worry, only regard me as your master and yourself as my slave. Only this much is needed, nothing else."

(Gītā 18.66)

Any neutral thinker can see that this theory reduces the moral strength of the human society. No society propagating such a line of thinking can raise the standard of its behaviour. This is why the moral standard of the people of India is continuously going down. People do not want to refrain from sin but want to avoid its fruit. And for this no austere *Sādhanā* is needed; only taking shelter with God or any of His incarnations is the highest *Sādhanā* which relieves one from distress. What is the value of life-long morality and good conduct where even prostitutes teaching their parrots to recite 'Ram' attained salvation, and where messengers of the Almighty Nārāyaṇa came rushing to take to heaven, life-long sinner Ajāmil who at the time of his death was simply calling his son Nârāyaṇ. Cheap devotion lowers down the importance of pious conduct. Thus the theory of descent based on such devotion creates among the people sense of irresponsibility; go on committing sin after sin and for escaping from their results take shelter with God.

The ideals of the theory of descent never adopt the form of reality worthy of being accepted by the people. So while hearing about the wonderful performances of the great men like Ram and Krishna when reference to any high ideal comes people suddenly exclaim, "Oh what can we say; it was God's performance; who else can perform such feats". Thus the followers of the theory of descent turn their face from all the superior and great qualities such as non-violence, compassion, charity, truth, benevolence etc. practised by our great predecessors and thus free themselves from the responsibility of observing them. According to the followers of the theory of descent all the great feats are the feats of God, not of men. They are only to be heard, not to be followed. Is it possible for a man to perform the feats performed by Almighty God ?

There are such references also as try to conceal the faults of the incarnation. When an enlightened thinker reads the biography of a person regarded as an incarnation and therein finds some moral fault then he criticises it and declares good as good and bad as bad. But the followers of the theory of descent deprive man of this right. Regarding such topics they generally say, "What do you know; it all is the *māyā* of the Almighty. Whatever he does, he does good, what we today declare as bad, in it also there might have been some good; we should have faith in God and should not calumniate him. Thus the descentists in the name of faith at once close the door of free thinking and examination of good and bad. King Parikshit was greatly perplexed when he heard the description of Krishna's free affairs with milk maids as described in the 10th Chapter of the *Śrīmadbhāgavata.* From such a wanton behaviour on the part of God he could not make out any thing. Then Śhukdeva puts forward a very queer logic. He says, "O King life of great men are only to be heard, not to be followed". No neutral thinker can be satisfied with this type of reconciliation. How can such great man whose life is only fit for being heard, not to be followed in the form of prescriptive or prohibitive rules be helpful in reforming our life ? Are the descentist writers motivating the public to follow the ideals resulting from the life of such great men ? If the answer to all these questions is given honestly it can be safely said that in the thinking of descentists except negative, there is nothing positive.

The ideal of *Śramaṇa* culture is the ascent of man, not the descent of God. In it the descent of God in human form is not accepted but, on the other hand, ascent of man to Godhood is accepted. Descent means—'coming down' and ascent means 'going up'. According to the *Śramaṇa* culture no other being is superior to man. Man is not simply a mobile skeleton made of bones and flesh but is a collection of endless powers. He is God of gods, self-proved God. But till the time he, on account of worldly infatuation and illusion, is covered with the dirt of action he is like the sun surrounded by *cloud.* In such a condition how can he give light ? Before being able to give light the sun has first to emerge from the thick cover of cloud.

As soon as a man comes to his senses, he realizes his real nature and giving up depended development comes to possess self-supported development. Then gradually, becoming stainless, pure and clean, he one day, as a collection of innumerable shining spiritual powers becomes pure and enlightened, Superior Soul, Arihant Brahma and God. In *Śramaṇa* culture the ultimate pure state of the soul is called God, the Supreme Soul. Besides this, there exists no other eternally perfect God.

This is the theory of ascent as propounded by *Śramaṇa* culture. It gives sublime motivation to man to become God on the strength of his own *Sādhanā.* It rouses man's spirit lying eternally dormant, develops and motivates it towards performing good actions. It does not discourage a man by saying that he is base and stupid. So the *Śramaṇa* culture teaches human beings to move forward towards the highest point of development.

*Śramaṇa* culture has been proclaiming for the last thousands of years that it does not at all believe in invisible and unknown God. For saying so, it received bitterest possible doses of reproach, insult, blame, admonition and hatred. But it did not deviate from its noble path. At every step it has ever been saying that no definite outline of the form of God is before us; he has since eternity been an object of mere hypothesis and has forever remained unearthly. What ideals can such a God place before us ? We can get nothing on the basis of his life and personality. Our ideal can be only such venerable divinity as has been himself a man like us, has been tortured by the wordly pleasures and pains, illusions and infatuations and later on, on the strength of his own *sādhanā* and spiritual awakening kicking off all the worldly luxuries and being free from all the bondage of action immune from passion and malice, has reached the ultimate spiritual objective i.e. deliverance.

Tīrthaṅkaras, Arihants, Jinas and the Siddhas, all were the *sādhakās* of this very type. They were neither unearthly divinities from the very beginning, nor the incarnation of god. Like us they were ordinary human beings of this world, besmeared with the dirt of sin and distressed by sorrow and pain, mental agony and diseases and enjoyment of pleasures of senses was their only aim. In search of such pleasures suffering, since eternity, various kinds of torture they had whirling in the hurricane of birth and death. But when they entered the path of spiritual *sādhanā* they realized, by means of Right View, the difference between the inert and the conscious and between physical and spiritual happiness and continuously observed *sādhanā* of self-control. In the course of many births, one day in the end, they were born as men and as the result of their self-*sādhanā* became Arihant, Jina and *tīrthaṅkara*. Even today in the religious works of the *śramaṇa* culture there are available many important examples of their ups and downs and the foot-prints of their successive religious practices prove that even in an ordinary man there exists the sprout of *Jinatva.* A man by sprinkling the water of his *Sādhanā* can develop it into a big tree and get the immortal fruit of *Jinatva.* The noble ideal of the life of the Arhats, victors of passion and malice, presents before the *Sādhaka* an outline for his successive progress and salvation. Thus the theory of ascent, as propounded by *Śramaṇa* culture is not only to be looked at but is to be brought in practice in all the stages of life. The theory of ascent motivates the humanity not to try to escape from the fruit of the sin but to escape from the sin itself, for the cause of lofty ideals of life, it kindles in the heart of the people an indestructible light of decayless, an immortal and endless noble courage.

# Anekāntavāda

**2**

*Upādhyāya Amar Muni*

*Anekāntavāda* is the foundation-stone of Jainism. The edifice of Jain philosophy itself stands on it. In fact, *Anekāntavāda* is the very life of Jainism. Whenever and whatever has been propounded in Jainism, it has always been done only after fully testing it on the touch-stone of *Anekāntavāda*.

The meaning of *Anekāntavāda* is to look at, to think over and to test every thing from different points of view. If we want to understand its real meaning we also call it *Apekśavāda*. In Jain philosophy looking at a thing only from one point of view is regarded as incomplete and unauthentic and looking at different properties of a thing from different points of view, is regarded as complete and authentic. This very way of looking at things is *Anekāntavāda*.

*Anekāntavāda* and *Syādvāda* are, like the two sides of a coin; two aspects of the same principle. This is why the common people regard these two as identical. But though they are outwardly one yet are basically different. *Anekāntavāda* is the speculative method of looking at a thing whereas *Syādvāda* is the way of its expression. Expressing the view-point of *Anekāntavāda* in language is *Syādvāda*. This means that *Anekāntavāda* is the pure and faultless method of thinking about the real nature of a thing and *Syādvāda* is to ascertain and disclose the secret of different ideas lying at the root of different properties of a thing. *Syādvāda* is also called *Kathanchidvāda*.

Jainism holds that each and every thing whether a minute particle of dust or the great Himālaya, is an assemblage of endless properties quality or speciality. For an example take a fruit. In it there is form, there is juice, there is smell, there is touch, there is shape and there is the power of satisfying hunger and also curing and producing so many diseases. Our wisdom is quite limited, so without possessing infinite knowledge, we cannot know about the endless properties of a thing. But we can definitely know, according to the power of our intellect, many of its clearly visible properties.

So we should not insist that by knowing a single property of thing we have known its complete nature. First look at the different aspects of a thing and only then say any thing about it. This is *Anekāntavāda.* It broadens our view-point and diverts the stream of our thinking towards completion.

In respect of a fruit when we say that it has also form, also juice, also smell and also touch, then we are following *Anekāntavāda* and *Syādvāda* and thus make a true assessment of the fruit. On the contrary, when we say that the fruit has only form; only juice, only smell and only touch, then we are following *Ekāntavāda,* which does not give correct assessment of the fruit. In 'also' note of acceptance of other properties of a thing lies hidden, whereas in 'only' there is clear negation of its other properties. 'It has form also' means that in the fruit along with the form there are also other properties such as juice, touch, smell etc. It has 'form only' means that in the fruit there is only form nothing like juice etc. The difference between 'also' and 'only' is the same as that between *Syādvāda* and *Mithyāvāda,* 'also' is the former and 'only' the latter.

A man is standing in the market. A boy comes from one side and addresses him as father; from another side comes an old man and addresses him as son; from the third side comes a middle-aged man and addresses him as brother and from the fourth side comes a student and addresses him as 'sir'. The same man is being addressed differently by different persons. They all start quarrelling among themselves saying that he is only father, only son, only brother and only teacher. Their clash comes to an end, when a *Syādvādī* comes and he says to the boy, "Yes, he is father to you as you are son to him; but he is not the father to others. He says to the old man, "Yes he is son only in your context, he is not son in the context of others." The meaning is that in the context of his son, he is father, in the context of his father he is son, in the context of his brother he is brother and in the context of his student he is teacher. So in view of changing contexts the same man may be uncle, nephew, husband and friend. A single man in different contexts has different properties. It is not that in the context of the same son, he is father, son, brother, teacher, uncle, and nephew. This is quite impossible and against the law of Natural philosophy.

To understand *Syādvāda* we further take another example. A man is sufficiently tall, so he says, "I am tall". When I ask him, "Are you taller than a mountain?" He at once replies, "No sir, I am shorter than a mountain. I was saying so in the context of my companions". There is another man. He is shorter than his companions. So he says, "I am short" When I ask, "Are you shorter than an ant?" He at once replies; "No sir, I am taller than an ant. I was saying so in the context of these tall companions".

From these examples the meaning of *Apekṣāvāda* must have been clearly understood. Every thing is short as well as tall. In the context of taller things, it is short and in that of shorter ones it is tall. In this way every thing has many aspects and to understand this point *Apekṣāvāda* should be applied. In philosophical language it is called *Anpekṣāvāda*.

For understanding *Anekāntavāda* our ancient teachers have given the example of an elephant. In a village there lived six congenitally-blind persons. Fortunately, one day an elephant came there. The villagers had never seen an elephant. So there arose great tumult. When those blind men heard about the arrival of an elephant they, too, ran to see it. They were blind, so they could not see the elephant. Every one of them started to feel it with his hand. One of them touched its tail, another its trunk, another its ear, another its tusk, another its foot and another its stomach. By touching only a part of the body of the elephant, every one thought that he had seen the whole elephant. When they came to their residence, they started talking about the elephant.

First of all, one who had caught its tail, said, "I have seen the elephant; it is exactly like a thick rope".

Then one, who had caught its trunk, spoke, "Absolutely false, it is never like a rope, it is like a pestle."

Then the third one, who had caught its ear, said, "If my eyes do not work it matters little. Hands can never betray. I touched the elephant with my hand, it is just like a winnowing basket."

Then the fourth one, who had caught its tusk, said, "All of you are giving false reports. The elephant is like a hoe".

The fifth one, who had caught its foot, said, "Fear God, why do you unnecessarily tell a lie. The elephant is like a pillar. I have thoroughly examined it."

Now the sixth one cried out, "Why do you talk non-sense ? You have become blind as the result of your previous sins. Now again by telling a lie, why are you committing further sin. I too, have seen the elephant, it is like a granary."

Fortunately there came a man having right vision. Seeing them quarrelling and using impolite language he began laughing. But the very next moment he became serious. He thought, 'To err is not a crime, but to laugh at the fault of others is definitely a crime.' His heart got filled with pity. He said, "Brothers why do you quarrel? Kindly hear me. All of you are right, none is wrong. None of you has seen the whole elephant. Only looking at the different parts of its body, you are describing the whole elephant. Do not call anybody a liar but try to understand the view-point of one another. From the point of view of the tail, it is like a rope, from the point of view of its trunk, it is like pestle, from the point of view of its ears, it is like a winnowing basket, from the point of view of its tusk, it is like a hoe, from the point of view of its feet, it is like a pillar and from the point of view of its stomach, it is like a granary, the blind men realised their mistake and being claimed down said, "yes brother you have rightly explained the point, different parts jointly constitute an elephant; a single part does not constitute it."

Actually the blind men having partially seen the elephant had begun to insist that they had seen the whole complete elephant. But when the man having right vision explained the point, then they realised their mistake and the quarrel ended.

All the sects in the world which follow *ekāntavāda* treat part of a thing as the whole and so quarrel with the persons of other sects. *Syādvāda* is an enlightened philosophy. So it explains to the blind followers of *ekāntavāda* that their thinking is valid from only one point of view, not from all the points of view. It is totally wrong to hold a part as true in all contexts and to reject other parts as false. Thus *Syādvāda* pointing out the mistake in the philosophies of *ekāntavāda*, presents the true form of a thing and says that every sect is right in a particular context. Thus it appeases the sectarian quarrel. Not only in the field of sectarian quarrel, if *Syādvāda* is applied in all the walks of life such as the family, the society and the nation then every where pleasant atmosphere of love and kindly feeling can be created. The seed of quarrel lies only in not understanding the view point of one another. *Syādvāda* is helpful in understanding the view point of others.

Till now, to understand *Syādvāda* only gross worldly examples have been given. Now the import of philosophical example also should be understood. As this topic is a bit serious, so it will be better to take recourse to the subtle method of observation.

Now we first take the question of eternal and transient itself. Jainism holds that every thing is eternal as well as transient. At this common people get bewildered as to how can eternal be transient and transient eternal. But Jainsim by means of *Anekāntavāda* easily solves this problem.

Suppose there is a pitcher. We see that it has been made with the same clay as other pots such as *sakorā* (cup made of baked clay) and *surāhi* (a long necked waterpot) etc. If we break the pitcher and present before any man another pot made of the same clay, he will never call it a pitcher. Though the clay belongs to the broken pitcher, yet what is the reason that the present pot is not called a pitcher. There is no other reason except that the shape of the present pot is not like that of the pitcher.

It proves that the pitcher is not an independent thing but only a particular form of clay. But this particular shape is not quite different from clay; it is only one of its forms, The clay itself has adopted different forms such as a pitcher, a *sakora,* a *surāhi* etc. So in this condition how can the different forms be absolutely different from it ? Thus it is clear that the shape of the pitcher and the clay both together give the pitcher its own form.

Now we have to see which of the two forms is perishable and which is constant. It is evident that the present form of the pitcher is perishable as it is created and so inevitably be destroyed. It did not exist before and shall not exist in future. In Jain philosophy it is called *paryāya.* And the clay, forming the pitcher, is imperishable because it never perishes. It existed before the pitcher was created, exists when the pitcher has been created and shall exist even after the pitcher is destroyed. Clay in its form of *pudgala* is a permanent element. It is neither created nor destroyed. In Jain philosophy it is called *dravya.*

On the basis of this discussion, it can be clearly understood that the form of the pitcher is perishable and the other one is imperishable; one is created and is destroyed, the other one ever exists, is constant. Thus from the point of view of *Anekāntavāda* we can say that the pitcher in the context of its shape is perishable and transient and in the context of clay, is imperishable and eternal. In the language of Jain philosophy the pitcher from the point of *paryāya* is transient but from the point of view of *dravya* is eternal. Thus *Anekāntavāda* proves the existence of apparently contradictory properties like eternity and perishability in the same thing.

The subject needs more thinking. All the things in the world have three properties; birth, existence and destruction. In Jain philosophy they are called *utpatti, Vyaya* and *dhrauvya.* It is also known as *tripadi*. You may ask how can mutually contradictory properties exist together in one and the same thing. To understand this point take an example. A goldsmith has a gold bracelet. He breaks it and prepares a necklace with it. A necklace is created but you cannot say that it is altogether a new necklace because the gold that existed in the bracelet still exists in the necklace, only the old shape has been destroyed and a new shape has been created. From this example all the three properties, destruction of the shape of bracelet, creation of the shape of a necklace and the constant existence of gold in both the shape, are well proved.

Thus the three qualities of birth, existence, and destruction naturally exist in every thing. When a thing is destroyed then it should not be thought that the original element in it has also been destroyed. Only its grass forms are subject to creation and destruction. Even after the destruction of the gross forms of a things its subtle molecules exist for ever. They in conjunction with other things create new forms. During the months of *Vaiśākha* and *Jyeṣṭha* when the rays of the sun heat the water of a tank then it is wrong to think that the water has become absolutely non-existent. That water still exists in the form of vapour or gas etc. Though its subtle form may not be visible to us yet it has not become absolutely non-existent. So this theory is immutable that neither a thing is totally destroyed nor from nothingness something positive comes into existence. Modern physics also supports this theory. It says, "Every thing in its original form is constant and stable and the visible things created from it are simply its different transformations."

The basic element that always exists in the three states, creation, existence and destruction in the Jainism called *dravya* and its states that are created and destroyed are called *paryāya*. In the example of the creation of necklace from bracelet, gold is *dravya* and the bracelet and the necklace are *paryāyas*. In the context of *dravya* every thing is eternal and in the context of *paryāya* transitory. Thus any thing is neither absolutely eternal nor absolutely transitory but is both eternal as well as transitory. To admit this is *Anekāntavāda*.

In respect of existent and non-existent *anekāntavāda* holds bipartite view. Many sects hold that a thing is absolutely existent. But as against it other sects say that a thing is also absolutely non-existent. Thus both the sides indulge in wordy quarrel. Only *anekāntavāda* can reconcile it in the right way. It says that every thing is both existent as well as non-existent; every thing also exists and also does not exist. In its own original form it exists, in other forms it does not exist. In the context of his son the father is existent but in the context of other's son he (a father) is non existent. If he be a father in the context of other's son also then he will be the father of the whole world. But this is absolutely impossible.

Before you there is a potter. Someone addresses him as goldsmith. He says that he is a potter, not a goldsmith. Though as a potter he is existent yet as a goldsmith he is non-existent. Suppose there are one hundred pitchers. As pitchers they all are existent. But from the point of view of such things as cloth etc. which are different from pitchers they are non-existent. Even every pitcher, too, is existent only owing to its quality and form but is non existent in the context of quality, property and form of other pitchers. There is difference also among the pitchers themselves. A man unknowingly picks up a pitcher, but when he sees it he says that it is not his pitcher, he places it back. In such a case the pitcher is not existent but is non-existent. The word 'not' in it indicates non-existence. Every thing is existent within its own limit, not outside it. Our personal form is the limit and the forms of others are outside the limit. If every thing in the world were existent in every form then there shall remain no law and order in the world. If milk is existent in the form of milk and also existent in the form of curd, in the form of whey and in the form of water, then everyone can give and take curd, whey and water in place of milk. Remember milk is existent only in the form of milk, it is non-existent in the forms of curd etc. because one's own form is existent but other forms are non-existent.

The immortal theory of *Syādvāda* has been regarded as a very lofty theory. Mahatma Gandhi has praised this theory without any reservation, western scholars like Dr. Thomas etc. also say, "The theory of *Syādvāda* is highly deep. It throws light on the different states of a thing."

In fact *Syādvāda* is the key to true knowledge. Today the predominance of enmity and clash concerning religion, society and nation all over the world, can be removed by means of *Syādvāda*. In the field of philosophy *Syādvāda* is such an emperor as coming before whom the vices of quarrel, jealousy, non-liberality sectarianism and narrowness etc., run away out of fear. All round auspicious reign of universal welfare can be established only by *Syādvāda*. This is an immutable and fast-fixed fact.

# Ideal Food

**3**

*Upādhyāya Amar Muni*

Food is essential for life. Without food human body cannot survive. But food is for life, not life for food. It is regrettable that at present food has become the sole aim of life. Man hankers after food. All the ancient rules regarding food and drink have been totally forgotten. Good or bad whatever comes before a man he consumes it. He hates neither meat nor wine. Presently a man running after taste does not care even for his health.

He starts eating as soon as he leaves his bed and like animals continues to eat throughout the whole day. He eats at home, eats at the houses of his friends and eats in the market. Thus he goes on eating till sun-down, sats at night and even while going to bed pours a glassful milk in his stomach, little caring for its capacity.

Ancient law-givers of India have prescribed highly useful rules in respect of food. In food attention is to be paid to purity, sanctity, cleanliness and health, not to taste. One should totally hate meat and wine which are not worth eating. Even whole some food is to be taken only when one feels hungry. In the absence of hunger eating even a single morsel of food is devouring sin. One should not eat more than twice or thrice a day. Taking food at night is improper from the points of view of religion as well as health.

In Jainism great stress has been laid on the prohibition of taking food at night. Not taking food at night is a distinctive mark of a Jain. Jainism holds that taking food at night is violence.

There are a number of such tiny insects as are visible only in the light of the sun. At night they are totally invisible. At night the light in our eyes gets dimmed. So when the tiny insects fall in our food and reach the stomach, they create havoc there. A man who has given up non-vegetarian food, he also is defiled by the guilt of taking non-vegetarian food. Thus the poor beings are ignorantly killed and the man's vow also is violated.

As against this some persons argue, "Taking food at night is prohibited only because tiny insects and moths are then not visible, so if we use electric light then there is no harm". But in the electric light the probable fault in taking food at night is not removed. Insects and moths encircling the electric light fall down in the food and unnoticed tiny insects enter our stomach along with food.

From the health point of view also taking food at night is to be given up. During the day heat of the sun helps in digesting the food. Further, if we take food during the day there is sufficient gap between taking food and going to bed. Thus the food gets ample time to be digested. Most of the people who take their meals at night go to bed just after taking their meals. In this way the food is neither fully digested nor juice is properly formed. Men taking food at night mostly suffer from indigestion and constipation and so many other diseases.

The root of renunciation lies in contentment. So from this point of view also food should be taken during the day along with other activities and at night we should contentedly give full rest to the stomach. In this way sound sleep is enjoyed, help is got in the observance of celibacy and their all-round health improves. This rule of Jainism is fully based on the spiritual as well as scientific point of view. In medical works also taking food at night has been said to be detrimental for health. At night heart and the navel lotus get shrunk and so the food is not well-digested.

Instead of delving deep into religious as well as medical works, if we simply consider the general harms caused by taking food at night even then it looks fully improper. If along with food, an ant is consumed wisdom is lost, if a louse is consumed the dangerous disease of dropsy is caused, if a fly enters the stomach vomitting takes place, if a lizard is eaten there is leprosy, if a scorpion enters along with vegetable, it pierces the palate and if hair sticks in the throat voice is damaged. In this way so many apparently visible diseases result from taking food at night.

Taking food at night is actully dangerous. Not one or two but thousands of tragedies result from it. Hundreds of people even lose their lives.

So taking food at night deserves from all point of view, to be given up. In Jainism it has been strongly prohibited. In other religions also it is not looked at with approval. In the *Kūrmapurāṇa* and other Vedic works also taking food at night has been prohibited. Mahatma Gandhi in the last forty years of his life, strictly abstained from taking food at night. Even in the Europe he never took his meals at night. It is the sacred duty of each and every Jain, to give up taking food at night; he should neither cook food at night nor eat it. Food we take should be strictly vegetarian.

We notice highly dreadful sins being committed in the world. But the sin of eating meat is most dreadful and censurable. Meat-eating destroys the tender feeling of the heart and renders it totally merciless and cruel. Meat is neither produced in fields nor grown on the trees nor rains from the sky. It is procured from the body of living animals by killing them. When a man cannot bear even the pain caused by a thorn in his foot and remains restless throughout then how for it is justifiable to cut the throat of innocent and dumb animals ? Think over it honestly and with cool mind, how great pain they might be experiencing, how abominal an act it is to kill other dumb animals for momentary taste. When a man is unable to grant life to anyone then what right he has to take anyone's life.

When even violence done to ordinary living beings in course of food and amusement is regarded censurable then to kill useful animals, our constant companions, is all the more dreadful. When the butcher lifting his glittering knife moves it on the neck of dumb animals, how dreadful that sight is. A kind man cannot even look at that monstrous sight. Stream of blood flowing, heaps of flesh being formed and blood-besmeared pieces of skin lying scattered here and there and vultures and kites etc. hovering over them. It is quite evident that in such a hateful situation only demons, not men, can live. This is why in Europe and other countries honourable judges do not accept butchers as a witness. In their eyes a butcher has grown so cruel that he ceases to be a human being. How can humanity and authenticity exist in a heartless and cruel man ?

In Jainism meat-eating has been strongly prohibited. Lord Mahāveer, the living incarnation of compassion, counts meat-eating among evil habits and treats it as the cause of hell. In the fourth *Sthāna* of the *Sthānāṅgasūtra* it has been said that the following four causes lead men to the hell : *Mahārambha. Mahāparigraha,* killing living beings having five senses and eating meat.

A certain preceptor derives the word *māṁsa* in a highly heart-touching way. He says the word *māṁsa* consists of two letters '*mām*' and 'sa'. 'Mām' means 'me' and 'sa' means 'he'; these two letters put together mean, "He whom I kill and eat, he will kill and eat me also". Meat-eaters should seriously think over this meaning and giving up the evil habit of eating meat save themselves from future miseries.

At present some people argue, "Is it not violence to grind thousands of grains and put them in the stomach ? In killing a goat only one living being is killed but in eating corn thousands of living beings are killed". The answer is that the original of wheat is water-based while that of the goat is urine-based. Wheat is a living being of indistinct consciousness whereas goat is a living being of distinct consciousness. Intention of the killer of a goat is apparently cruel, merciless and violent but a wheat-eater's intention is not so. So equating a goat with grains of corn, not only indicates ignorance but also mental cruelty. A polluted, hateful and malignant thing like meat can never be equated with pious corn.

Meat-eating is also against human nature. Man is by nature vegetarian, not non-vegetarian. There is a great difference between their formation. Nails of non-vegetarian animals such as dogs, cats and lions etc. are pointed and sharp but those of vegetarian ones like elephants, cows and buffaloes etc. are not so. Further the jaws of non-vegetarian animals are long whereas those of the vegetarian ones are round. By looking at the faces of the cow and the dog the difference becomes obvious. Non-vegetarian animals drink water lifting it with their tongue and vegetarian ones with the support of their lips. By looking at cows, buffaloes and monkeys etc. on the one hand, at lions, cats and dogs on the other hand, this difference becomes clear. Vegetarian animals like cows, horses and camels etc. perspire whereas non-vegetarian ones like cats, lions and leopards do not.

Modern science has proved that monkeys and gibbons are totally vegetarian. They life-long live on fruits and flowers. Man's external as well as internal formation resembles those of monkeys and gibbons. So man also is fully vegetarian. Habit of eating meat he has acquired from external perversions. It is not in harmony with his original nature.

From the economic point of view also meat-eating is harmful. Cows, buffaloes, goats etc. are greatly useful for the country. How dreadful it is to kill them? It deserves our attention.

For example let us take a cow. Economists have calculated that from a cow we get milk, curd, clarified butter, bullocks and cowdung etc. and one complete generation of a cow provides happiness to 4,72,600 people. Biologists after serious investigation have calculated that the mean of the milk given by each cow is eleven kilograms. The average period of her giving milk is twelve months. Thus with the milk given by each cow in her life-time 24,960 people are satisfied for one time. Every cow gives birth to six heifers and six calves. Even if one from each group dies then by the milk of the remaining five heifers given in their life-time 1,24,800 people at a time can be satisfied. The five bullocks in their life-time produce at least two thousand quintals of corn. If each man consumes three quarters of a seer of corn then normally two and half lacs of people can for one time fill their belly. With the quantity of milk given by heifers and the corn produced by bullocks the hunger of 3,74,800 people can be satisfied for one time. Putting both the figures together, from one generation of a cow 4,75,690 people are nourished for one time.

Not only this much. Bullocks pull carts and are also used for riding and carrying loads. This is why Indians address the cow as 'mother'.

Similarly with the milk given by one she-goat in her life time 25,920 people can be nourished for one time. Elephants, horses camels and sheep etc. also help men in many ways. Thus those men who kill such useful animals or get them killed by others are murderers of the whole human society.

From the health point of view also meat is to be a prohibited thing. Usually from meat-eating diseases like cancer, tuberculosis, pyorrhoea, gout, headache, epilepsy, insanity, insomnia, paralysis and gallstone etc. are produced. Physical strength and mental sharpness also are adversely affected. By scientific experiments conducted in this context in the University of Brussels in Europe, vegetarians have been proved better than non-vegetarians. Ten thousand students participated in the above mentioned experiment. Out of them five thousand were given only vegetarian diet like fruit, milk and corn etc. and the remaining five thousand were given non-vegetarian diet. After six months when they were examined, it was found that the vegetarians were in all respects better than the non-vegetarians. In the vegetarians the qualities of compassion, forgiveness and love appeared and in the non-vegetarians anger, cruelty and cowardice were seen. Qualities like strength and forbearance etc, were found more in the vegetarians than in the non-vegetarians. In vegetarians mental power also had developed better.

In short from all the points of view, religious, social, economic and health, meat-eating is highly censurable. A man entitled to be called a man, should give up meat-eating for ever.

# Service to Humanity

*Upādhyāya Amar Muni*

4

Though Jainism lay great emphasis on retirement, penance and endurance, yet its ideal is that men should mutually serve and help one another and according to their capability and strength help others. In Jainism the very characteristics of the individual soul is regarded as socialistic, not individualistic. Every man, in his individual form is imperfect, his perfection depends on the society around him. This is why Jain culture gives equal importance to spiritual practices as well as service to villages, towns and the nation. In Jainism man's duty towards villages, towns and the nation has been regarded as *dharma*. Lord Mahāveer also in his religious sermons accords a very high position to duty towards village, towns and nation. He places the *Sādhanā* of spiritual and ritualistic Jainism after service not before it. None else but only a civilized citizen and patriot can be a true Jain. In the light of the above statement how can it be said that Jainism gives top preference to retirement or its aim is the other world, not this world. Jainism does not bank on credit (future) but on cash (present). It gives us noble impetus to make glorious this as well as the other world.

A Jain householder getting up in the morning thinks over three points. First of all he earnestly resolves to spend all his wealth over the service of the people, he thinks that blessed shall be the day when his collection would be utilized for the poor and the afflicted. Lord Mahāveer proclaims : It is the duty of a man not to regard only himself as entitled to utilize his collection but also regard his neighbours as equally entitled to it. One who utilizes his resources for himself alone and does not bestow on others even something from it, he can never break his bondage and obtain deliverance.

Among the eight basic actions accepted in Jainism the nature of *mohanīyakarma* (the action which enamours the soul) is highly awful. No other action causes so much downfall of the soul as this. Its final and the violent form is called *mahāmohanīya-karma.* Out of its thirty types, the twenty fifth one is, "If your friend is ill or is in some great trouble and you are able to help or serve him yet you do not help him thinking that as he has never helped you, then why should you help him; if he is suffering let him suffer, it in no way concerns you". In this context Lord Mahāveer in his sermon at Champāpurī clearly says, "One who is indifferent to his duty, falls headlong from *dharma* on account of the sin of his above-mentioned cruel line of thinking. He for a long time, till seventy *kotākatī sāgar* remains entangled in the cycle of birth and death and not be ever able to realise the truth".

Not only the householders but even the ascetics have to strictly perform the duty of service. Lord Mahāveer says, "If an ascetic leaving his ailing and afflicted campanion starts observing penance and gets engrossed in spiritual thinking, he incurs guilt and so does not deserve to live in the order. He has to undergo the expiation of one hundred and twenty fasts failing which he can never be purified. Further if in a village an ascetic is ill and another ascetic even knowing about his illness, does not come to the village for nursing him but continues going from one village to another, he too, is guilty and deserves severe punishment". Lord Mahāveer further says, "Service itself is a great penance". So when-ever the sacred opportunity of serving others is got it should not be missed. He is a true Jain who with a view to serving others is always in search of afflicted poor, fallen and down-trodden persons.

The *Sthānāṅgasūtra* refers to eight well-known great teachings of Lord Mahāveer. The fifth one is, "Help him, shelter him and make proper arrangement for maintaining him who is helpless, without any support and has no proper resources for his maintenance". The doors of a Jain householder ever remain open for every helpless person. Irrespective of caste, clan, country and creed he respectfully provides shelter to all human beings.

There is one thing more of great importance which greatly raises the position of service. In Jainism a *tirthaṅkara* holds the highest and the most important position. As soon as the *sādhaka* becomes a *tirthaṅkara* he turns a great man. Superior even to gods, he is worshipped by the masses. Both Lord Pārśvanāth and Lord Mahāveer were *tirthaṅkaras.* Lord Mahāveer in his last sermon stressing the importance of service says, "It is by service alone that the position of *tirthaṅkara* is achieved." For instilling the importance of the service in the mind of the masses this elevated sermon of Lord Mahāveer is highly efficacious.

Āchārya Haribhadra and Kamalsamyama present before us a very beautiful dialogue between Lord Mahāveer and Gautama. There the Lord regards the service to the people as superior to service to him. The dialogue runs thus, Indrabhuti Gautama, the senior-most *Ganadhara* of Lord Mahāveer once asked him, "Lord! one devotee serves, worships and prays you day and night. As a result of this he gets no time to serve the poor and the afflicted. Another devotee serves the poor and the afflicted, helps them and identifies himself with their service. As a result of this he does not get time to serve you. O Lord! which of the two is superior and object of your thanks" ?

The Lord replied in an awakening tone, "O Gautama! one who serves the poor and the afflicted is superior; he alone is the object of my thanks and is my true worshipper". Gautama began to think what is this in relation to the service to the Lord, what is the importance of serving the sinners, suffering on account of their own evil actions. He alone, who serves the Lord actually deserves thanks. Gautama asked in an inquisitive tone. 'Lord I could not make out any thing. Serving you should be more important than serving the afflicted. On one side you, the Lord of all the three worlds, and on the other the sinful persons suffering the result of their own actions'.

The Lord replied, "True service to me lies in obeying my orders. Besides, my personal service I give no credit at all. My other is that the afflicted masses should be provided happiness and peace; pity be shown to all living beings. Thus one who serves the afflicted actually obeys my order. O Gautamas, so I say that blessed and superior is he who serves the afflicted and not he who serves me. One who serves me is entangled in delusion, is not following the true principle of service."

Thus the service to the people is equal to service to the *Jina*. This sermon of Lord Mahāveer, the last radiant sun of the Jain culture is the clearest testimony to the importance of service.

When Lord Mahāveer decided to renounce the world, he liberally donated his wealth for the welfare of the poor subjects and also postponed for one year his decision to undergo initiation. He considered it his prime duty first to donate his huge wealth for the service of the people. Before bringing about spiritual upliftment of humanity, he remained engrossed in the work of its physical advancement. Even after initiation boundless ocean of compassion overflowed in his heart. As a result his heart got filled with pity at the wretched condition of a poor *brāhmaṇa* and he gave away to him his only scarf.

Emperor Chandragupta, a true follower of Mahāveer also did not lag behind in the field of service. His works of public welfare are well-known. Emperor Samprati's services to the people are in no way less. Even an ordinary student of Jain history knows as to what extent sentiment of service to the people was filled in his heart and how he brought it into practice and kept intact the glory of Jain culture. Kharavela, the king of Kaling and Kumarpal, the king of the Gurjaras, always maintained the dignity of the Jain culture in the field of service. In medieval age business magnates like Jagadushah, Pethad and Bhamashah also sacrificed their everything for the welfare of the people and themselves became indigent like a cloud after it has rained.

To assess the services of the Jain community to the people, there is no need of going through the past history. Visiting Gujarat, Mārwār, Mewād or Karnataka and looking at the ruins of houses, reading the inscriptions on the stone-slabs of the mountains and hearing the common report in the villages one can know what Jain culture actually is and how close relation it has with service to the people. Jain culture is not connected with an individual but with the whole society. The meaning of cultured society is that it be saturated with the sentiment of maximum service; no envy but love, no duality but identity, and uniform living as one family. Glorious and bright as of Jainism is a true witness to the existence of this great ideal of culture. The present Jain community should preserve the glory of its great past and in the present difficult condition of India, irrespective of the differences of caste, creed and clan and come as a pioneer in the field of service to the poor and regard it as the true service to God.

## Dāna

There are thousand and one ways of helping humanity. But the most effective and efficacious way is fourfold *Dāna* (charity). Besides, helping the poor and the needy, it also lightens the burden of excess wealth from head of the richman and thereby leads him to earn virtue. In India great importance has been attached to religion. Even the most ordinary matters are tested on the touchstone of religion. There are countless number of religious activities. All the noble thoughts and practices form the part of religion.

But as regards the highest religion great men hold different views. Some regard penance as the highest religion, some compassion, some truth, some devotion to God, some celibacy and some forgiveness. All of them are right from their points of view. But in my opinion charity is the highest religion. Its importance is very great. It destroys misfortune, makes the human heart generous and large, rouses the sleeping humanity, causes to flow the Ganga of compassion and love in the heart of the people and prepares a beautiful and fragrant atmosphere of sympathy. By giving charity nothing remains unattainable in the world. A charitable man gets love and respect every where. The fragrance of his fame spreads in all directions.

Giving charity is not so easy. Giving away one's amassed wealth to anyone gladly and with open mind, is really an act of great courage. People quarrel and even die over each and every penny, endanger even their life. Only after moving heaven and earth a few chips are earned. Ten vital airs have been mentioned in the religious works. People regard wealth as the eleventh vital air. This is why it has been said to give and to die are equal. Spending one's hard-earned money for the sake of benevolence is possible only for fortunate and divine souls. Those men and women who give charity without any selfish motive and remain happy after giving it, are really divine persons. While giving charity the giver touches a very great height in life.

In Jainism glory of charity has been greatly sung. The donor is said to be entitled to get heaven and even *Nirvāṇa*. Lord Mahāveer himself was a great donor. He loved to give charity from his very childhood. Whenever he saw a poor man, tears of compassion rolled down from his eyes. At that moment whatever he had, he gave it away to him. Lord Mahāveer was a prince. There was no dearth of any kind of material pleasure. He normally took his meals only after distributing it among his companions. After renouncing the throne when he was ready to become an ascetic then also he distributed charity continuously for one year. What ever wealth he had, he donated all for the service of men. Those days he daily donated one crore and eight lacs gold coins. Lord Pārshvanāth and other *tīrthaṅkaras* also were great donors. Among conduct, penance and other forms of religion, charity has been given the first place.

In Jain works four kinds of charity have been mentioned : 1. Giving food, 2. Giving Medicine, 3. Giving knowledge, and 4. Giving protection.

## Giving Food

Food is the first need of a living being. When he is hungry, he understands nothing. Food is the vital air of life. One who gives food is supposed to have given everything.

Food is to be given, with humility and devotion to the world-renouṇcing ascetics coming to one's house. Giving food to true ascetics *Nirjarā* of most of the sinful acts is attained.

Giving food to hungry poor men is also a great religious and pious act. King Pradeshi, being influenced by the preachings of Keshi Kumar, a Jain ascetic, arranged to spend one-fourth part of his royal income over the poor. Jainism which has a feeling of universal pity accepts as its prime duty to be a cosharer in the sorrow and pain of the people and to help them.

## Giving Medicine

An ailing person is good for nothing. He can neither feed himself nor his family nor can faithfully practise religious rites. When he is mentally well then alone all the religious practices are possible. Mental health usually depends on bodily health. When a man is ill he feels great sorrow and becomes restless. In this very way all living beings feel sorrow and pain. So in Jainism great importance is given to giving medicine to the ailing.

Āchārya Amitgati, in his *Upāsakāchāra* says, "The importance of giving medicine is beyond description. On the administration of medicine when a man regains his health he gets for the time being happiness like Lord *Siddha.* The Āchārya has given this example from the point of view of health. Lord *Siddha* is regarded healthy from the spiritual point of view and a worldly man is regarded healthy from the material point of view. On regaining health there comes peace which alone provides true happiness.

Another deep-sighted Jain Saint while enumerating the kinds of happiness says, "The first happiness is the healthy body." Disease-free condition of the body is regarded as the happiness *par excellence.* It is quite right that when a man gets indisposed nothing interests him; then food, drink, sweet words and merriment taste like poison. Then medicine alone gives him the highest happiness. When a sick man recovers after taking medicine, he showers profuse blessings. This alone gives happiness and peace to him.

## Giving Knowledge

Without knowledge man is blind. If a blind man gets back his vision how happy he is; in the same way imparting knowledge to an ignorant man is very important. Giving knowledge has been compared to donating eyes.

In ancient times universities like Nalanda etc, were established with this very sentiment. Thousands of students from various parts of India as well as from abroad such as Syam, Java, Sumatra, China, Turki and Greece received education here without any distinction of caste, creed and country. To open schools for the poor students, to give donation to schools, to award scholarships, to give books etc. and to build boarding houses, all these are included in giving knowledge. Jainism has played important role in this field also. Āchārya Amitgati has gone so far to say, "All the four objects of man's creation *dharma, artha, kāma* and *mokṣa* are achieved through knowledge. So one who imparts knowledge is entitled to achieve all the four." Lord Mahāveer also says, "First knowledge; pity, penance and benevolence etc. afterwards."

## Giving Protection

Giving protection means to save a dying man and also to rescue one fallen in distress. This has been regarded as the best form of charity. *Shri Sudharmasvāmi,* the first successor of Lord Mahāveer, says, "Amongst all types of charity giving protection is the best one."

Giving protection is the very life-blood of Jainism. Its foundation itself lies on it. Āchārya Amitgati in his *Upāsakāchāra* says, "The happiness that a living being feels on getting protection can be gained in no other way."

A kind man achieves the position of God. Lord Mahāveer also achieved the position of God only by giving protection. He neither himself inflicted pain on anyone nor caused other do so. Not only this much. He devoted his total life to protect the dumb animals to be slaughtered at the time of sacrifices etc. The main reason behind the disappearance of horse-sacrifices and such other murderous sacrifices from India was the result of Lord Mahāveer's efforts based on the principle of giving protection.

So it is the duty of each and every Jain to help by all means, the distressed beings, rescue the dying beings, save by giving food and drink the life of persons starving to death, make proper arrangements for serving the dumb cattle by constructing cowpens and cow-houses and to utilize the maximum part of his wealth in the work of kindness to the living beings. In the present violence-pervaded epoch if the Jains do not come forward to perform the ideal work of causing to flow the Ganga of compassion, then who else can do it. Wheresoever and in whatsoever condition a Jain be he should everywhere create an atmosphere of non-violence and compassion. He alone is a true Jain by getting whose affection even the face of a distressed man flowing tears beams up for the time being with the sweet smile of happiness. Wheresover a Jain be he should be known as a giver of life.

These four kinds of charity are only to indicate its scope in general. It is not limited to this much only. Whatsoever action makes others happy, it comes within the purview of charity. Lord Mahāveer while explaining virtue says, "By giving food, water and clothes a man attains the virtue which gives happiness like heaven etc." The Jain literature is full of thousands of examples indicating the importance and great fruit of charity. In this connection the stories of Kayavanna Seth, Śalibhadra and Dhannā Seth etc. are quite well known. The present discussion in respect of charity is for opening the eyes of those who say, "Jainism is an idle religion. It limits itself only to penances and renunciation. It does not provide such preachings as lead to public welfare." Any right thinking man can well see that the above detailed discussion regarding charity proves activeness of Jainism, not its idleness. The line of thinking in respect of charity has placed Jainism unrivalled in the field of the works of public welfare.

One or two questions regarding charity greatly need our consideration. Some people say, "Charity is the most virtuous act. But only a worthy person is entitled to get it and that worthy person is none but an asectic. So charity to any poor and distressed worldly person, other than an ascetic is sin, not virtue. All the wordly people are unworthy of charity and charity to such persons is the cause of worldly bondage."

This hypothesis in respect of charity is quite illogical. Not only an ascetic is worthy of charity even such house-holders as lead virtuous life are worthy. To regard only ascetics as worthy is to distort the meaning of the *Śāstra.* Any man leading a virtuous life is worthy. And again no where it is laid down that charity is to be given only to a worthy person, not to any poor or distressed person. Lord Mahāveer also accepts charity as the main characteristic of Jainism. On the sight of any distressed person with compassion in the mind make efforts, to help him is true charity. No doubt charity to a worthy person has great importance but when a distressed person comes then to think over his worthiness or otherwise is not the true form of charity. Jainism has come on the earth with an intention to bring welfare to all living beings. It does not want to confine the wave of compassion arising in the human heart, within the narrow limits of any particular caste, country, sect, creed or person. If a poor man comes before us and in the hope of a piece of bread extends his hands, he is a worthy to get some thing from a well off man. It is not human to leave the poor man to remain rotting in the adverse situation created by privation. Authenticity of charity to the poor and the distressed can never be questioned.

There is one more argument against giving charity to the hungry and the poor. A few philosophers say, "Charity is not to be given to a lame, a decrepit, a poor and a leper etc. because they are the victims of God's wrath. He is punishing them for their sins. As such taking pity on them and helping them is in a way interfering with God's systems of punishment. If God punishes a man for his sins it is proper to let him suffer."

These so-called wise men hold that God will be displeased if we interfere in his work. Jainism holds that the very principle that God punishes anybody is in itself wrong. God is absolutely free from attachment and malice. He has no business to punish the poor beings. To describe God as the inflictor of punishment is to find an excuse for not fulfilling the duty towards the distressed beings.

Even if God is punishing a person, we should try to save him. Jainism cannot stop helping the distressed even if God himself comes before him and forbids to help the poor. A man should always hear the voice of humanity arising in his heart and be ready to wipe off the tears of the poor. A true Jain is the friend of the poor; in all conditions he shall help him.

# Āchārya Mahāprajña : A Living Legend

5

*Muni Prashant Kumar*
*Muni Lokprakash 'Lokesh'*

Over the centuries, philosophers and intellectuals have appeared on this planet who have influenced humanity and whose thoughts have continued to guide and stimulate generations after generations and even change the course of social progress. In the field of science, the contribution of the likes of Newton, Faraday or Hinstern can never be forgotten. The names of Freud, Burgson and Jung in the field of psychology or Marx in socialism would ever remain shining. In the field of spirituality, Mahāvīr, Buddha, Christ, Śankarāchārya and many others have moulded the lives of countless followers of the spiritual path but in the current times, Āchārya Tulsī has become a household name for propagating the gospel of humaneness, nonviolence, brotherhood and 'Anuvrat'. His chief disciple and now the Āchārya (Tulsī having renounced it voluntarily and passed on the mantle during his own life-time to Mahāprajña) Mahāprajña, as a pragmatic thinker, preceptor and a blender of spirituality and science, has also become a living legend. While the entirely new precepts, principles and perceptions of Āchārya Mahaprajña have enlightened the intellectuals, he has also carved a permanent place as a philosopher-saint in the hearts of the masses by his concrete proposals to improve the quality of life and living. The new vistas opened up by him in the field of spirituality would serve as a light-house to the tossing *mahāyāna* (ship) of mankind for centuries to come.

In this century, it was Swami Vivekanand who had emphasised the harmonious synthesis of science and spirituality for the first time, which some years later was reinforced by Mahatma Gandhi and Vinoba. Āchārya Mahāprajña has further crystallised this thought through his writings in which both spirituality and science have been projected as mutually complementary. His stand that far from destroying religion, science has in fact revived it, is an entirely new concept in religion. The credibility of this proposition was further confirmed by him with practical tips in the art of living. 'Prekshadhyan' (Perceptive meditation) is one such dimension of this concept. By looking inward and with detatchment, spirituality no more remains either dry or supernatural subject but becomes an attractive proposition for even a common man. The various scientific methods of 'Prekshadhyan' not only projected the 'Dharma' in an entirely new perspective but it also became an integral part of one's daily life. This was nothing less than a miracle in the religious world and a new perception gained ground that religion without science is in fact lame and cannot gain necessary confidence of the people. But science without religion is also blind. This was also propounded by Einstein some years back. It cannot get a meaningful direction without spiritual awareness and without the latter, could also be used for destruction, annihilation and perverting perceptions.

In the sublime proximity of Gurudev Tulsi, Āchārya Mahāprajña has invented the 'Prekshadhyan' procedure for the spiritual and moral development of the individual. By adopting this, tens of thousands of people have liberated themselves from their mental tensions and have commenced their lives' journey on an entirely new path. The scientific process of Prekshadhyan has proved unique for the wholesome development of an individual's inner consciousness and his entire personality. It is said that the hardened aptitudes or attitudes of a grown up man, normally cannot be hanged. There is a saying that neem (a tree whose leaves and fruits are bitter in taste) leaves cannot be sweetened, even if the tree is irrigated with butter and honey. The Prekshadhyan procedure has demolished this time-tested theory. On the basis of many experiments and surveys, it can now be conclusively stated that by this procedure, not only significant changes occur in the individual physically but his mental and emotional attitudes and apptitudes are also transformed and his past habits changed.

On the directions of his spiritual mentor Ganādhipati Tulsī, the Āchārya undertook an intensive study of the Jain 'Agam' scriptures and through an indepth study of meditation processes, he also systematised them by providing a scientific basis. Before presenting Prekshādhyān procedure to the people in an organised manner, Mahāprajña subjected his own body to many a trial and tribulation of meditation processes. As a recluse for months together and even in the jungles, he lost himself into sustained reflections whereby his inner powers were awakened. With his reaching the unfathomable depths of meditation, many mysteries, hitherto unknown, began to unfold themselves before him. Ganādhipati Tulsī then inspired and encouraged him in this unique experiment and on the 3rd March 1977, when Mahāprajña undertook one such exercise of long seclusion, the former wrote to the later "This experiment is not yours alone but mine also as also of the Sangh (Sect). The whole Sangh will be benefitted by it."

By diving deep into the depths of contemplation. Mahāprajña has supplied us with many a jewel. 'Chaitanya Kendra Prekhsha' (Perception of Psychic Centres) and 'Leshyadhyan' (Perception of Psychic colour) procedures of Prekshādhyān are the fruits of his innate vision. Albert Einstein was once asked as to how he invented the Theory of Relativity. His spontaneous reply was that it had just happened to him and he could not say how it happened. It is the same story with Mahāprajña. He thinks, ponders and deliberates upon a particular subject, issue or problem and when he cannot find a solution, leaves that problem alone and then suddenly during his morning meditations, a crystal clear solution, evading him till now, springs up before him. This is possible only when one transcends the realm of mind or intellect and enters the realm of intuition which is an innate faculty of one's own consciousness/psyche.

During the initial training course camps, many renowned intellectuals, thinkers and social workers also participated and as of date, thousands and thousands of persons of all castes and creeds, sects, classes or areas have gained from 'Prekshadhyan'. Lord Mahāvīr and thereafter some Jain saints had also practised it, but this mode of contemplation gradually disappeared and the credit of reviving it goes to Āchārya Mahāprajña and thus many intellectual commentators justifiably call him the 'Columbus of Jain Meditation'.

The Āchārya is both a thinker and a genius and his horizons are all-pervasive. He is deeply concerned with day-to-day life and also social, national and international problems and thinks aloud about all of them. Significantly, he not only presents the problems but also simultaneously provides their solution. He first gives deep and sustained thinking about the possible remedies before placing them before the people.

About the problems of modern education, it appealed to him that mere literacy or even knowledge does not necessarily develop the individual's total personality. With intellectual development through higher education, a person does not automatically develop morally, emotionally and spiritually. Many educated depressions are found involved in crime, violence or other immoral activities. In fact, in the elaborately pre-planned economic scams or other crimes or violence or treason, it is the educated persons who are mostly involved. In the absence of proper emotional development, such reprehensible activities are only natural because in a person devoid of tender feelings like love, compassion, tolerance, patience, contentment, altruism etc., it is only futile to expect any moral development or humane behaviour and conduct. It would therefore not be surprising if such a person then indulges in violence, crime, rape or other unethical activities/or even suicide.

Today's education has therefore failed to fulfil the expectation society has from it. Its aim should be to build up the human being but despite manifold increase in the number of higher educational institutions like colleges, universities etc., the criminal and beastly tendencies of man are on an increase. Why ? This entire educational system today is the butt of every shaft and charges are being freely levelled that modern education and its procedures cannot bring about any social transformation.

In this context, Āchārya Mahāprajña has formulated the concept of 'Jeevan Vigyan' (Science of Living) as a panacea for this universal problem. Both Ganādhipati Tulsī and Āchārya Mahāprajña have stated that the modern education cannot be dubbed as entirely faulty because it has produced such innumerable doctors, engineers, lawyers, judges, bureaucrats and administrators, who have excelled in their respective fields and have added to the nation's glory and whose name and fame have travelled beyond the national boundaries. Therefore, today's education, though otherwise useful is in fact inadequate. It equips the individual to earn his livelihood but not in the art of living. In today's education, while there are ample avenues for physical and intellectual development, it does not necessarily provide for mental and emotional development. There is no technique or mode in the input of current educational system which may control and mitigate human perversions like cruelty, jealousy, selfishness, vengeance, fear, hate or lust—it does not provide for any specific training programmes for the students to control their anger, rashness or other impulses detrimental to his proper development. In order to achieve this, Ganādhipati and Āchārya, in their concept of the 'Science of Living' made specific provision of a comprehensive syllabii and training courses for students and many scientific tests were formulated whereby the internal transformation gradually occurring in a student could also be monitored.

It is now a well accepted theory that the internal bio-chemicals affect our thoughts and behaviour. The endocrine hormones intereact with the nervous system and many functions of the latter are thereby balanced and coordinated. In extremely adverse circumstances, when tension aggravates, it puts additional, sometimes unbearable, pressure on the endocrine system thereby disrupting the existing balance between the sympathetic and the parasympathetic nervous systems. In such a situation, the sympathetic nervous system gains the upper hand, which is the root cause of many negative emotions even in educated and intelligent persons. By the proper functioning of endocrine system, the sympathetic and parasympathetic nervous system also remain balanced whereby a person can find a satisfactory solution of his inner problems and resist the onslaughts of external pressures. The 'Science of Living' is a singular experiment in this creation.

The main objective of the 'Science of Living' is threefold. First, to build such a healthy personality which could maintain equilibrium in its physical, mental, emotional and social health. Second, to build such a new society which is free from violence, exploitation and immorality and third, to build such a new generation which has a spiritual-cum-scientific personality.

The training courses and practices enunciated by Mahāprajña, which a student has to undergo, results in crucial bio-chemical and bio-electrical changes in him which ultimately transform him. But, this procedure does not preclude the existing syllabi meant for the students' intellectual development. The former, in fact, only supplements the latter. About value-oriented education, the Āchārya further says that mere preaching this procedure would not suffice and the student must be made to go through various exercises and experiments and to periodically repeat them in order to kindle his desire to lead a value-oriented life. A mere command to any tree to supply sweet, succulent fruits would be meaningless. Sow the proper seed first. As you sow, so shall your reap, provided the seed is nurtured by proper air, manure and watering.

Besides being a thinker and a genius, Āchārya Mahāprajña is also an excellent writer and a poet. His brain-storming penmanship has stirred countless readers and intellectuals throughout the length and breadth of this country. Admirers of his writings range from the common man to literary personalities, sociologists, journalists and political leaders. On wide-ranging subjects like Logic, History, Philosophy, Poetry, Grammar, Yoga, Spiritualism, Travelogue, Reminiscences, Biography and current topics, the Āchārya has written more than a hundred books, many of which have also been translated into English, Gujarati, Tamil, Telugu, Kannada and Bangla languages and also one or two in German and Japanese.

Despite being overladden by serious thoughts, his literature has attracted even the common man. This is because he practises what he preaches and his perceptions, besides being original, are also crowned with concrete remedies proposed for various problems. His exceptional trait is that his intellectual excellence permeates the very grandeur of his actions. He does not restrict his thoughts only at the thinking level but wants their consummation into actual conduct. Every individual is engulfed in some mental (either imaginary or circumstance-based) problem or the other, and he craves for some proper diagnosis and a possible cure. Āchārya's literature provides him precisely what he wants and thus his books which are a craze, have gone into many editions. The renowned Bangla novelist, late Vimal Mitra once said, "I discover new truths from Mahaprajña's writings. When I read him, it appears that while I write for the people, Mahāprajña is writing for me. Alas ! Only if I had read him during my initial formative years, the course of my own literature would have been entirely different." Atal Bihari Vajpai, an eminent political leader says, "I am a lover of Mahāprajña's literature and am overwhelmed by it." A renowned poet, late Rāmdhāri Singh Dinkar said, "Mahāprajña is the modern Vivekānand. We never saw Vivekānand but only read and heard about him. But we do see him now in Mahāprajña." Jainendra Kumar, a renowned writer and thinker, says, "Detatched thinkers like Mahāprajña are rare. His sweet temperament and deep thinking inspire me to sit with him for as long as possible."

Mahāprajña is gifted with that rare acumen which is free from any prejudice or preconceived notion and his tackling of a problem is always comprehensive. His all-pervasive assessment is clearly reflected in the 'Jain Agam (classical) Literature' edited and critically annotated by him. By this colossal work, he has facilitated the permanent preservation of many thousand years' old canonical scriptures and has embellished them with a scientific outlook acceptable to the people. This old literature is in 'Prakrit' language and its commentaries are available either in 'Prakrit' or 'Prakrit mixed with Sanskrit'. Mahāprajña first undertook their deep, sustained study and only thereafter commenced the gigantic herculean work of editing them and through sheer talent and insight, provided their new meanings and interpretations. Through sheer strenuous work day and night for many years continuously, the original text of the thirty-two Agam Scriptures was determined and their Hindi translation also completed. Detailed commentaries thereon made them more interesting and comprehensible to the people. This awesome task carried out in accordance with the verbal renderings by Ganadhipati Tulsi was guided by an entirely non-sectarian and open mind and is therefore viewed with respect by the heads of other sects as well as intellectuals and oriental scholars of the East and the West. This difficult huge work which otherwise would have cost crores of rupees, was accomplished under the editorial direction of Mahāprajña by the self-less and dedicated service of a team of talented saints (both male and female) paying their homage to this sacred cause in the shape of their hard intellectual work.

Mahāprajña also wrote a Sanskrit commentary (Bhaśya) on Āchārang Sutra, the oldest and most incomprehensible Jain scripture and thereby revived and reestablished a very old tradition of elucidation of holy literature.

While meeting Mahāprajña, one gets the thrill of meeting the 'Spiritual India' or the 'Wonder that was India' to borrow the words of Dr. A.L. Basham. While reading him, one gets the sensation of flowing in a river, a river which though initially is a mere rivulet but as one goes along it swells into a big river spreading its bed encompassing a huge territory and occasionally hands over some sparkling pearls or some flowers of indescribable fragrance, which the reader wants to permanently preserve. His language as also his style is endearing and creates an instant rapport with the reader and keeps him engrossed even in subjects otherwise deep, serious and dry.

Besides being a philosopher-thinker lost in philosophy, he is also a sensitive poet. His verses both in Hindi and Sanskrit, reveal his subtle, delicate feelings. In Sanskrit, he is also an expert impromptu or extempore poet and has demonstrated this rare skill in many gatherings of intellectuals and of general masses also. Poetry has in fact seeped into his entire life. As a poet, it is difficult to categorise him into a type. Is he a poet of torrential waves of ecstasy or renunciation, a singer of the Nature's beauty or its monstrosity or of the man in the clutches of machine, mechanisation or machinations, nobody can tell. His wings as a poet are all-encompassing and reach territories hitherto unexplored. His sensitive dynamism is not confined to any specific area but reach and quench the thirst of even the distant deserts of man's mind. *Sambodhi, Ashruvina, Mukulam* (all in Sanskrit) and *Rishabhayana* (in Hindi) are some of the literary jewels contributed by him to the world of literature.

His narration of the life of Lord Mahāvīr reads like an engrossing novel. In his book '*Śraman Mahāvīr*', he has woven the fabric of Prince Mahāvīr's life who renunciated the luxuries of a palace and went away to the jungles for his penance and then this saint prince also went to the tribal areas, where the tribals harassed and harmed him. Mahāprajña depicts Mahāvīr from the depth of his meditation and in such a way that he seems to come alive to the readers.

His epic '*Sambodhi*' represents the soaring heights of his poetic capacities. The rhythmic conversation between Lord Mahāvīr and the Prince-Monk Megha Kumar, in fact unties many a knot of life and philosophy. Another book, '*Rishabhayan*' (now being completed) also gives a glimpse of his maturity as a poet. His poetry is illuminated by the divine light of life's philosophy. He is a blossomed rose of inner refinement whose fragrance pervades not only through his verses but also the spoken words. The crowds which regularly throng around him, are enthralled and get peace in his presence as he is also in peace with himself.

Mahāprajña's favourite topic is mind. Majority of the man's problems would be resolved with the resolution of problems of mind; individuals usually get perturbed, even unbalanced, due to adverse circumstances. To them, Mahāprajña's advice is that instead of functioning like the slipping and flowing water, one's mind should be solidified like ice and should remain so, as if kept in a refrigerator. The dirt, dust falling on it, will then slip away and will not stick while in the water; these are bound to assimilate and also pollute it. Similarly, all outside dirt in the form of tension, unhappiness etc. seep into only a slippery, shifting mind but when the mind is stable, tensions etc. shy away without affecting it.

The story of Mahāprajña's ascendance to the pinnacle of spiritual and intellectual development commenced when he was just a child of 10 years. Born in Tamkor (A very small village in District Jhunjhunu, Rajasthan) on 14th June 1920 and baptised as 'Nāthmal', this child, on 2nd January, 1931, renunciated the family and worldly pleasures and started on the thorny path of asceticism. He was taken as a disciple by Āchārya Kalugani, the eighth Āchārya of Terāpanth of Jainism and the child dedicated his whole being at the feet of his Master. Āchārya Kalugani then entrusted this child to the care of his young and talented disciple Muni Tulsi and by his simplicity and unaffectedness, the child instantaneously endeared himself to his new teacher. With Muni Tulsi, the child's intellectual development got accelerated and he memorised thousands of sermons and verses in Hindi, Sanskrit, Prakrit and Rajasthani. He also expertised in long, extempore discourses in Sanskrit and made an indepth study of Jain scriptures. A study of History, Philosophy. Logic, Grammar etc. made the foundations of his knowledge strong and secure. He also made an indepth study of Modern Physics and Bio-Sciences, Āyurved (Indian system of medicine), Politics, Economics, and Sociology with the modern trends of Communism, Socialism and Capitalism and gradually became a leader of all the senior and talented saints of Jainism. His fame now travelled far and wide throughout the country and his speeches and writings became the talking point amongst the people and his discourses have often been organised in various colleges, universities and centres of learning.

When Muni Tulsī ascended the Āchāryahood, he started the 'Anuvrat' Movement, in which Muni Nāthmal was associated from the very beginning and by giving it a philosophical content, Muni Nāthmal made an original contribution to the Movement, not confined to any caste or creed but covering the entire humanity and he also emphasised Anuvrat's usefulness and relevance the people in the present context.

From Kachh (Gujrat) to Calcutta and from Punjab to Kanyakumari, Mahāprajña undertook the historical 'Padyātra' (travel on foot) with the Anuvrat Anushasta Tulsi. During these travels, he addressed thousands of public meetings and conveyed the message of unity, brotherhood and nationalism. He was the centre of attraction and thousands of people used to throng to hear him.

He dispelled many myths about religion and its rites and rituals. He said, "The religion which does not bring about a change in a man's life, which does not impart peace to him deserves to be thrown into the river Ganges rather than carried on as burden on one's shoulders. Rituals or idol worship alone are not enough unless one's conduct also gets transformed. Religion is not confined only to temples, mosques or churches, but extends to the man's day-to-day living as well." According to him in India, out of nearly 90 crores of people, only 6 to 7 crores consider themselves to be non-followers of any religion, but the remaining 83 crores people do profess themselves as religious. But are they indeed religious ? Unless one is also righteous and honest, both to himself and to others and leads a value-oriented life, he is not religious despite his proclamation to the contrary. And, for bringing about an ultimate transformation from within and modifying the whole life-style, Mahāprajña's Prekshādhyān course has been adopted till date, by thousands of people.

On 12th November, 1978, in view of his hallowed vision, intellect and genius, Āchārya Tulsi endowed Muni Nāthmal with the qualitative epithet of 'Mahāprajña' and on 4th February 1979, his appellation 'Mahāprajña' was converted into his new name and he was also made 'Yuvacharya', successor designate to the present Āchārya, the second highest position after the Āchārya himself. For his exceptional and sustained contribution to the cause of 'Jain Yoga' the epithet of 'Jain Yoga Ke Punruddharak' (Reviver or Resurrector of Jain Yoga) was also conferred on him.

In a mammoth public meeting on 18th February 1994, Anuvrat Anushasta Tulsi declared that Mahāprajña would now have the title of 'Āchārya' also and that the former was renouncing this position forthwith. Subsequently, on 5th February, this year, Mahāprajña was formally consecrated as the 10th Āchārya (the Supreme head) of Terāpanth religious order in a big public meeting in Delhi. It is an unprecedented event of history, where a renowned, talented and competent Āchārya suo-moto abdicated his position in his own life-time and entrusted it to his successor.

The implicit rapport between Ganādhipati and Āchārya is astonishing. All along, the latter has been and continues to be completely dedicated to the former. Accumulation of knowledge and arrogance usually go together. But Mahāprajña symbolises that fruit-laden tree which, due to the weight of its own fruits, is bowing down. His knowledge wears the crown of humility. Even after issuing to the Āchāryahood, his dedication and devotion to Ganādhipati Gurudev Tulsī, remains undiminished. Anybody could see, nay, feel the transparent sincerity and simplicity oozing from Mahāprajña. The affection and confidence of Ganādhipati in Mahāprajña is also beyond description. People doubt if there ever was such a unique team of master-disciple.

Tulsī and Mahāprajña are two in form, one in spirit.

Acharya Mahāprajña is fortunate in having taken over the reins of 'Terāpanth' in the life time of his own preceptor. Due to this leadership of one of the most disciplined religious organisations, Mahāprajña is now burdened with many responsibilities. Further intensification of the Movements of Anuvrat, Prekshādhyān and Jeevan-Vijñan is now his primary concern; the forum of Terāpanth would now be more actively involved in propagating these movements for the renaissance of society. A 'Vikash Parishad' (Development Council) has recently been constituted by Mahāprajña to play an important role and give further fillip to all these movements. The Terāpanth, nay, the whole Jain Community is proud of and overwhelmed by the elevation of Mahāprajña as their Tenth Āchārya.

The deep understanding of Āchārya Mahāprajña enables him to look beyond Time. He can anticipate the needs and expectations of the coming era. Instead of getting entangled with problems he looks for their solution. Those who know him intimately are aware that he is the creator of new perceptions. He is the blending artist of heart and wisdom on the one hand and thought and action, on the other. Impressed by his competence, capacity and calibre, many learned persons say, "It is a result of the penance of Shri Tulsi, during his present and previous lives that he was gifted with a disciple like Āchārya Mahāprajña."

Ganādhipati Tulsī himself is proud of such an able successor. Not only the Jain Community but the entire humanity has tremendous expectations and hopes from this rare personality. May he live for more than a century and serve as a beacon for the guidance of mankind.

# The Jain Declaration on Nature

6

*L. M. Singhvi*

The Jain tradition which enthroned the philosophy of ecological harmony and non-violence as its lodestar flourished for centuries side-by-side with other schools of thought in ancient India. It formed a vital part of the mainstream of ancient Indian life, contributing greatly to its philosophical, artistic and political heritage. During certain periods of Indian history, many ruling elites as well as large sections of the population were Jains, followers of the *Jinas* (Spiritual Victors).

The ecological philosophy of Jainism which flows from its spiritual quest has always been central to its ethics, aesthetics, art, literature, economics and politics. It is represented in all its glory by the 24 *Jinas* or *Tirthankaras* (Path-finders) of this era whose example and teachings have been its living legacy through the millenia.

Although the ten million Jains estimated to live in modern India constitute a tiny fraction of its population, the message and motifs of the Jain perspective, its reverence for life in all forms, its commitment to the progress of human civilization and to the preservation of the natural environment continues to have a profound and pervasive influence on Indian life and outlook.

In the twentieth century, the most vibrant and illustrious example of Jain influence was that of Mahatma Gandhi, acclaimed as the Father of the Nation. Gandhi's friend, Shrimad Rajchandra, was a Jain. The two great men corresponded, until Rajchandra's death, on issues of faith and ethics. The central Jain teaching of *ahiṁsa* (non-violence) was the guiding principle of Gandhi's civil disobedience in the cause of freedom and social equality. His ecological philosophy found apt expression in his observation that the greatest work of humanity could not match the smallest wonder of nature.

## The Jain Teachings

### *Ahiṁsa* (non-violence)

The Jain ecological philosophy is vitually synonymous with the principle of *ahiṁsa* (non-violence) which runs through the Jain tradition like a golden thread.

> "*Ahiṁsa parmo dharmaḥ*" (Non-violence is the supreme religion).

Mahāvira, the 24th and last *Tirthankara* (Pāth-finder) of this era, who lived 2500 years ago in North India consolidated the basic Jain teachings of peace, harmony and renunciation taught two centuries earlier by the *Tirthankara* Pārshva, and for thousands of years previously by the 22 other *tirthankaras* of this era, beginning with Ādinātha Rishabha, Mahāvir threw new light on the perennial quest of the soul with the truth and discipline of *ahiṁsa*. He said :

> "There is nothing so small and subtle as the atom nor any element so vast as space. Similarly, there is no quality of soul more subtle than non-violence and no virtue of spirit greater than reverence for life."

*Ahiṁsa* is a principle that Jains teach and practise not only towards human beings but towards all nature. It is an unequivocal teaching that is at once ancient and contemporary. The scriptures tell us :

> "All the *Arhats* (Venerable Ones) of the past, present and future discourse, counsel, proclaim, propound and prescribe thus in unison : Do not injure, abuse, oppress, enslave, insult, torment, torture or kill any creature or living being."

In this strife-torn world of hatred and hostilities, aggression and aggrandisement, and of unscrupulous and unbridled exploitation and consumerism, the Jain perspective finds the evil of violence writ large. The teaching of *ahiṁsa* refers not only to wars and visible physical acts of violence but to violence in the hearts and minds of human beings, their lack of concern and compassion for their fellow humans and for the natural world. Ancient Jain texts explain that violence (*hiṁsa*) is not defined by actual harm, for this may be unintentional. It is the intention to harm, the absence of compassion, that makes action violent. Without violent thought there could be no violent actions. When violence enters our thoughts, we remember *Tirthankara* Mahāvīra's words :

> "You are that which you intend to hit, injure, insult, torment, persecute, torture, enslave or kill."

## *Parasparopagraho jivanam* (interdependence)

Mahāvīra proclaimed a profound truth for all times to come when he said :

> "One who neglects or disregards the existence of earth, air, fire, water and vegetation disregards his own existence which is entwined with them".

Jain cosmology recognises the fundamental natural phenomenon of symbiosis or mutual dependence, which forms the basis of the modern-day science of ecology. It is relevant to recall that the term 'ecology' was coined in the latter half of the nineteenth century from the Greek word *oikos,* meaning 'home', a place to which one returns. Ecology is the branch of biology which deals with the relationships of organisms to their surroundings and to other organisms.

The ancient Jain scriptural aphorism *Parasparopagraho jivanam* (All life is bound together by mutual support and interdependence) is refreshingly contemporary in its premise and perspective. It defines the scope of modern ecology while extending it further to a more spacious 'home'. It means that all aspects of nature belong together and are bound in a physical as well as a metaphysical relationship. Life is viewed as a gift of togetherness, accommodation and assistance in a universe teeming with interdependent constituents.

### *Anekāntavāda* (the doctrine of manifold aspects)

The concept of universal interdependence underpins the Jain theory of knowledge, known as *anekāntavāda* or the doctrine of manifold aspects. *Anekāntavāda* describes the world as a multifaceted, everchanging reality with an infinity of viewpoints depending on the time, place, nature and state of the one who is the viewer and that which is viewed.

This leads to the doctrine of *syādvāda* or relativity, which states that truth is relative to different viewpoints (*nayas*). What is true from one point of view is open to question from another. Absolute truth cannot be grasped from any particular viewpoint alone because absolute truth is the sum total of all the different viewpoints that make up the universe.

Because it is rooted in the doctrines of *anekāntavāda* and *syādvāda,* Jainism does not look upon the universe from an anthropocentric, ethnocentric or egocentric viewpoint. It takes into account the viewpoints of other species, other communities and nations and other human beings.

### *Samyaktva* (equanimity)

The discipline of non-violence, the recognition of universal interdependence and the logic of the doctrine of manifold aspects, leads inexorably to the avoidance of dogmatic, intolerant, inflexible, aggressive, harmful and unilateral attitudes towards the world around. It inspires the personal quest of every Jain for *samyaktva* (equanimity) towards both *jiva* (animate beings) and *ajiva* (inanimate substances and objects). It encourages an attitude of give and take and of live and let live. it offers a pragmatic peace plan based, not on the domination of nature, nations or other people, but on an equanimity of mind devoted to the preservation of the balance of the universe.

### *Jiva-dayā* (compassion, empathy and charity)

Although the term *'ahiṁsa'* is stated in the negative (*a* = non, *himsa* = violence), it is rooted in a host of positive aims and actions which have great relevance to contemporary environmental concerns.

*Ahiṁsa* is an aspect of *dayā* (compassion, empathy and charity), described by a great Jain teacher as "the beneficent mother of all beings" and "the elixir for those who wander in suffering through the ocean of successive rebirths".

*Jiva-dayā* means caring for and sharing with all living beings, tending, protecting and serving them. It entails universal friendliness (*maitri*), universal forgiveness (*ksamā*) and universal fearlessness (*abhaya*).

Jains, whether monks, nuns or householders, therefore, affirm prayerfully and sincerely, that their heart is filled with forgiveness for all living beings and that they have sought and received the forgiveness of all beings, that they crave the friendship of all beings, that all beings give them their friendship and that there is not the slightest feeling of alienation or enmity in their heart for anyone or anything. They also pray that forgiveness and friendliness may reign throughout the world and that all living beings may cherish each other.

## Jain Cosmology

Jains do not acknowledge an intelligent first cause as the creator of the universe. The Jain theory is that the universe has no beginning or end. It is traced to *jiva* and *ajiva*, the two everlasting, uncreated, independent and co-existing categories. Consciousness is *jiva*. That which has no consciousness is *ajiva*.

There are five substances of *ajiva* :

*dharma - the medium of motion
*adharma - the medium of rest
*ākāś - space
*pudgala - matter
*kāla - time

*Pudgala* (matter) has form and consists of individual atoms (*paramāṇu)* and conglomerates of atoms (*skandha*) which can be seen, heard, smelt, tasted and/or touched. According to Jains, energy, or the phenomena of sound, darkness, shade, heat, light and the like, is produced by conglomerates of atoms.

The *jiva* (soul) has no form but, during its wordly career, it is vested with a body and becomes subject to an inflow of karmic 'dust' (*asravas).* These are the subtle material particles that are drawn to a soul because of its wordly activities. The *asravas* bind the soul to the physical world until they have brought about the karmic result when they fall away 'like ripe fruit' by which time other actions have drawn more *asravas* to the soul.

With the exception of the *Arihantas* (the Ever-Perfect) and the *Siddhas* (the Liberated), who have dispelled the passions which provide the 'glue' for the *asravas,* all souls are in karmic bondage to the universe. They go through a continuous cycle of death and rebirth in a personal evolution that can lead at last to *mokśa* (eternal release). In this cycle there are countless souls at different stages of their personal evolution : earth-bodies, water-bodies, fire-bodies, air-bodies, vegetable-bodies and mobile bodies ranging from bacteria, insects, worms, birds and larger animals to human beings, infernal beings and celestial beings.

The Jain evolutionary theory is based on a grading of the physical bodies containing souls according to the degree of sensory perception. All souls are equal but are bound by varying amounts of *asravas* (karmic particles) which is reflected in the type of body they inhabit. The lowest form of physical body has only the sense of touch. Trees and vegetation have the sense of touch and are therefore able to experience pleasure and pain and have souls. Mahāvīra tought that only the one who understood the grave demerit and detriment caused by destruction of plants and trees understood the meaning and merit of reverence for nature. Even metals and stones might have life in them and should not be dealt with recklessly.

Above the single-sense *jivas* are micro-organisms and small animals with two, three or four senses. Higher in the order are the *jivas* with five senses. The highest grade of animals and human beings also possess rationality and intuition (*manas*). As a highly evolved form of life, human beings have a great moral responsibility in their mutual dealings and in their relationship with the rest of the universe.

It is this conception of life and its eternal coherence in which human beings have an inescapable ethical responsibility, that made the Jain tradition a cradle for the creed of environmental protection and harmony.

## THE JAIN CODE OF CONDUCT

### The five *vratas* (vows)

The five *vratas* (vows) in the Jain code of conduct are :

* non-violence in thought, word and deed,
* to seek and speak the truth,
* to behave honestly and never to take anything by force or theft,
* to practise restraint and chastity in thought, word and deed,
* to practise non-acquisitiveness.

The vow of *ahiṁsa* is the first and pivotal vow. The other vows may be viewed as aspects of *ahiṁsa* which together form an integrated code of conduct in the individual's quest for equanimity and the three jewels (*ratna-traya*) of right faith, right knowledge and right conduct.

The vows are undertaken at an austere and exacting level by the monks and nuns and are then called *mahā-vratas* (great vows). They are undertaken at a more moderate and flexible level by householders and called the *aṇu-vratas* ('atomic' or basic vows).

Underlying the Jain code of conduct is the emphatic assertion of individual responsibility towards one and all. Indeed, the entire universe is the forum of one's own conscience. The code is profoundly ecological in its secular thrust and its practical consequences.

## Kindness to animals

The transgressions against the vow of non-violence include all forms of cruelty to animals and human beings. Many centuries ago, Jains condemned as evil the common practice of animal sacrifice to the gods. It is generally forbidden to keep animals in captivity, to whip, mutilate or overload them or to deprive them of adequate food and drink. The injunction is modified in respect of domestic animals to the extent that they may be roped or even whipped occasionally but always mercifully with due consideration and without anger.

## Vegetarianism

Except for allowing themselves a judicious use of one-sensed life in the form of vegetables, Jains would not consciously take any life for food or sport. As a community they are strict vegetarians, consuming neither meat, fish nor eggs. They confine themselves to vegetable and milk products.

## Self-restraint and the avoidance of waste

By taking the basic vows, the Jain laity endeavour to live a life of moderation and restraint and to practise a measure of abstinence and austerity. They must not procreate indiscriminately lest they overburden the universe and its resources. Regular periods of fasting for self-purification are encouraged.

In their use of the earth's resources Jains take their cue from "the bee [that] sucks honey in the blossoms of a tree without hurting the blossom and strengthens itself". Wants should be reduced, desires curbed and consumption levels kept within reasonable limits. Using any resource beyond one's needs and misuse of any part of nature is considered a form of theft. Indeed, the Jain faith goes one radical step further and declares unequivocally that waste and creating pollution are acts of violence.

## Charity

Accumulation of possessions and enjoyment for personal ends should be minimised. Giving charitable donations and one's time for community projects generously is a part of a Jain householder's obligations. That explains why the Jain temples and pilgrimage centres are well-endowed and well-managed. It is this sense of social obligation born out of religious teachings that has led the Jains to found and maintain innumerable schools, colleges, hospitals, clinics, lodging houses, hostels, orphanages, relief and rehabilitation camps for the handicapped, old, sick and disadvantaged as well as hospitals for ailing birds and animals. Wealthy individuals are advised to recognise that beyond a certain point their wealth is superfluous to their needs and that they should manage the surplus as trustees for social benefit.

The five fundamental teachings of Jainism and the five-fold Jain code of conduct outlined in this Declaration are deeply rooted in its living ethos in unbroken continuity across the centuries. They offer the world today a time-tested anchor of moral imperatives and a viable route plan for humanity's common pilgrimage for holistic environmental protection, peace and harmony in the universe.

# Banking and Currency in Ancient India

7

## (As depicted in Jain Canonical Literature)

*D. C. Jain*

Banking plays an important part in the modern economic activities. The different productive agencies, be they extractive dealing with the farm, the mines and the forests, or manufacturing converting raw materials into finished products, or transport carrying men and materials from one place to another, are all directly concerned with banking and look to it for credit and other facilities. Even an ordinary person has a link with a bank either as a depositor or a borrower of money.

### Banking in Ancient India

Coming to the ancient India i.e. about two and a half millennium ago, we find banking in its rudimentary state. Institutional banking was non-existent. Individuals looked after it. It was just like indigenous banking of today. It can be studied under the following heads:

1. Loanable Funds
2. Lending of Money
3. Receiving of Deposits

### Loanable Funds

References in the texts show that the rich and wealthy persons (Sresthis and Vaniyas) carrying on business amassed huge wealth which they used for three main purposes. The first purpose was to hoard a portion of the wealth to be used in time of need. The second was to use the money in business as capital and multiply it. It also included lending of money on interest. The third purpose was to use the wealth for fulfilling the personal wants comprising necessities, comforts and luxuries. The Upasakadasaga Sutram mentions ten Gathapaties who were bestowed with rich fortunes and had a huge wealth which they used for triple purpose of hoarding, investing and spending. The first Gathapati, Ānanda of Vaniyagama had total wealth of twelve crore Hiranya (gold coins).[1] He boarded one-third of the amount, i.e. four crore 'Hiranya' as reserve (Nihana) and spent another one-third in meeting his expenses over articles of needs and luxuries. The remaining one-third i.e. four crore 'Hiranya' (gold coins) was used for lending and investment in business in order to multiply the sum.[2]

Thus the rich Gathapatis and Sresthis earmarked a portion of their wealth for investment in business and lending purpose. The Bhagavatisutra mentions the well to-do Sravakas (house holders) of the town of Tungika, who increased their wealth by banking business. (Aoga-dvigunadi vrdhya artha pradhanam).[3] Generally one-third of the wealth was set apart by the Gathapatis for investment and loan purpose. Narration in Upasakadasanga Sutram shows that all the ten Gathapatis invested about one-third of their wealth in business which included money lending.

## Lending of Money

Money lending was considered as an honest business. The Vanikas gave money to the people on loan.[4] The loan was given in the presence of a witness or a surety (Śākśi or pratibhu).[5] Interest charged was generally heavy and sometimes it was as high as to make the principal double (duguna) every year.[6] Though there were prescribed limits to the interest chargeable by the lenders,[7] it was not very much followed. The State ordinarily did not interfere in matters concerning money lending. This must have caused untold misery to the borrowers who were at the mercy of rapacious usurers charging very high rates of interest. The Vanikas treated the debtors mercilessly for non-repayment of loans. They even whipped them to get their money back.[8] The debtors unable to repay the debts were made to work as slaves (anaya).[9] The Pinda Niryukti describes how a widow who purchased some oil from a merchant had to serve as a slave-girl on account of non-payment of the price of the oil.[10] The slaves had to work hard in the fields and workshops of their creditors. Sometimes, however, the debtors were relieved after a partial payment of the debt. It is stated that if the debtor (*dharniya*) went abroad and due to ship-wreck or other calamity returned home without any money, he was not liable to repay the loan.[11] This means that repayment of loan advanced for foreign trade depended on the safe return of the merchant with his cargo and sale proceeds. Thus, there was an element of insurance too, in such advances.

References in the texts show that loan was granted both for consumption and for production purpose. The rich and affluent Sresthis and Gathapatis described as saviour of the people must be advancing money to the needy persons for their trade and callings. In Jñatadharmakathanga Sutram we find Dhanya Sarthavaha announcing to advance money to the needy traders who were willing to accompany the Sartha (caravan of traders) for trading purposes.[12] There is mention of Sarthavahas of Rayagiha (Rajagir) who lent money with a view to double their principal.[13]

## Receiving of Deposits

Receiving of deposits is an important function of banking. A banker is one who besides lending money, receives deposits. In ancient days we find this function also being discharged by the Sresthis, Vanikas and Sarthavahas. People reposed confidence in these persons and deposited their money with them for safe custody. The money thus deposited was called 'Nikkhevaga'[14] They got back their money on demand. Of course, in some cases the depositors had to return home with a wry face when the banker (Vanika) refused to recognise him as a depositor. Instances are to be found when the Vanikas misappropriated the whole deposit (Nikhevage) and the poor depositors found themselves helpless.[15]

We can say that depositing money with Vanikas was not safe and as such it is not surprising that people kept their surplus money with themselves and hoarded them underground (nihi).[16] The dishonest bankers were a great stumbling block in the development of banking in ancient India. In the absence of adequate and secured banking facilities, trade and industry could not get full support to make a marked headway in those days. The usurious rate of interest coupled with dishonest practices thwarted the growth of banking in ancient India.

We also find that there was no specialisation in banking business. A lender advanced loan to persons for various purposes *e.g.* agricultural, industrial, trading or for consumption purposes. He must have been primarily guided with the return of his money and interest. In certain cases, the lender also lent with a view to promote agriculture, industry or trade in the country. Thus, the idea behind lending was two fold-first, to get interest and secondly to help develop the economic activities. But by and large the main intention was to multiply their capital by charging high rate of interest. However, it is proved beyond doubt that banking constituted one of the economic activities in ancient days and it did help in carrying on economic activities.

## Currency

The use of currency by the people anywhere at any time suggests the existence of a government. The maintenance of law and order is the prime requisite for the safe transmittance of currency from one place to another. The canonical texts mention the use of coins made of gold, silver and copper.

### Issue of Coins

The State had the power and responsibility of manufacturing and issuing coins. However, there are evidences to show that some of the Srenis (guilds) also minted and issued coins.[17] The Srenis took active interest in developing trade and commerce and it seems that the coins were first introduced by the Srenis (trade guilds) and the goldsmiths. Coins found at Taxila bear the word 'Nigama' which proves that the Srenis (nigamas) issued coins.[18]

In the beginning the administration was indifferent on this issue and the issue of coins was continued by the Srenis for a pretty long time. Eventually, with the growth of trade and commerce and growing circulation of coins, the State was tempted to issue coins and thus, both the king and the Srenis undertook this work. Hence, it can be safely said that the issue of coins was never a State monopoly at that time.

## Methods of Manufacturing Coins

We find that the coins at that time were manufactured by two different methods. The first mode of fabrication was to beat out a piece of metal (generally silver) into a flat plate of certain thickness and then cut off narrow strips of about half an inch or more in width. Each strip was then cut into separate equal sized pieces which were brought down to a fixed weight by cutting small bits off one or more corners of the pieces.[19] Different symbols were then stamped on the surface of the metals. Such coins were punchmarked coins. The second method of manufacturing was to shape the metals in moulds. The coins thus manufactured were cast coins.

## Punchmarked Coins

The punchmarked coins were the earliest coins of India. It is difficult to say precisely how old were these coins. These were certainly current in the time of Lord Mahāvīra i.e. in the sixth century B.C.[20] Sir A. Cunningham has no difficulty in thinking that they might mount as high as 1000 B.C. He says,

"They certainly belong to the very infancy of coinage. The only money that could have preceded them would have been black pieces of silver, which were weighed out."[21]

The punchmarked coins were called 'kahavana'[22] (karsapana) from 'Karasa', the weight, and 'apana', the custom or the market.[23]

In the beginning these coins were small flat pieces of silver either square or round adjusted to a certain fixed weight of somewhat more than 56 grains.[24] The Hindus and the Buddhist literature also frequently refer Karsapana. The copper Karsapana weighed so rattis which was equal to 144 grains.[25]

Several hoards of punchmarked coins have been found at different places in India, for example, at Taxila, Mathura, Eran (old decayed city on the south bank of river Bina, 45 miles north west from Sagar), Kausambi, Rajagṛha, etc. The coins bear different symbols on the obverse side such as a bull or a cow, a tree, a square tank, a snake, a peacock, an elephant, a palm tree, a lotus flower, a female figure, the moon, the sun, etc. The different symbols were probably the private marks of ancient coin fabricators. The number of these symbols are so great, nearly three hundred, that their origin was probably due to several different causes.[26]

The reverse side of the coins was left blank at the time of fabrication and gradually punched with different symbols at different times. The punchmarked coins are generally found in silver and copper. The coins found in hoards are largely in silver which indicate their larger use in those times. Gold Karsapanas might also have been issued like silver and copper ones. Their non-discovery is not a decisive argument against their existence.[27]

## Cast Coins

Cast coins were also manufactured in gold, silver and copper and contained different symbols like the punchmarked coins. The die of their manufacture was engraved with different symbols which produced the desired type of coins. A large number of copper cast coins of ancient India have been found at different places viz. Taxila, Ayodhya, Ujjain, Eran, Banaras, etc.[28]

## Types of Coins

Different types of coins (Nanaka)[29] prevalent at that time may be studied under the following heads :

(a) Gold coins

(b) Silver coins

(c) Copper coins

(d) Other coins

## Gold Coins

Among the gold coins 'suvanna' (suvarna) or 'dinara'[30] and 'suvanna masaka' have been mentioned. The words 'hiranna' and 'hirannasuvanna' also occur in the texts. The term 'hiranna' denoted money in general but when associated with suvanna (i.e. hiranna-suvanna), it meant gold coins.[31]

Suvanna or Dinara was the gold coin commonly used in eastern India (puvvadesa). The mention of "Pitamnama-Suvarna tanmayamva nanakam bhavat, yathapurva dese Dinarah"[32] certifies its use. Another coin known as 'Kevadika' has been mentioned which was possibly of gold and was in circulation in puvvadese (Eastern India).[33] The Jaina texts have made no distinction between the value of Suvanna and Dinara and as such they may be treated at par. On the basis of evidences of the Kusāna and Gupta coins also, a suvarna (Suvanna) had a value equal to that of the Roman gold coin, 'Dinarious' and it weighed 123 grains.[34] According to others the 'suvarna' weighed 16 masa (80 rattis) which is equivalent to 144 grains.[35]

'Suvannamasaka' (Suvannamasaya) was the smaller denomination of Suvanna or Dinara. This gold coin weighed only one masa (5 rattis).[36]

## Silver Coins

Among the silver coins 'Ruvagas' (Rupakas) have been generally mentioned in the texts. It seems that it was the most popular silver coin of the time. We find different regions having ruvagas of different values with different names. For example; the ruvaga of Diva Island[37] was called 'Diviccaga' or Sabharaga', that of Uttarapatha, 'Uttarapahaga' of Pataliputra, 'Padaliputtaga' or Kasumapuraga' of Dakkhinapatha, 'Dakkhinapahaga' and of Kancipuri 'Nelao' or 'Nelaka'.

The relative value of different ruvaga (silver coins) of the regions can be ascertained from the following table :

| | | | |
|---|---|---|---|
| 2 | Sabharaga or Diviccaga | = | 1 Uttarapahaga.[38] |
| 2 | Uttarapahaga | = | 1 Padaliputtaga |
| | and | | |
| 2 | Dakkhinapahaga | = | 1 Kancipuri Nelaka |
| 2 | Kancipuri Nelaka | = | 1 Ruvaga of Kusumanagara (Padaliputtaga)[39] |

Thus, it appears that the Pataliputra ruvaga was of highest value among the silver coins in as much as one Padaliputtaga (coin) was equivalent to two ruvagas of Uttarapatha and to 4 Diviccaga. Similarly one Kusumanagara (Pataliputra) coin equalled 2 Nelakas (Kanchipuri) or 4 ruvagas of Dakhinapatha.

Another silver coin mentioned is 'Dramma' which according to commentary on Bhat Kalpa Sutram, was prevalent in Bhillamala[40] (Bhinamala in District Jodhpur).

## Copper Coin

Copper coins seem to be prevalent in large number at that time. The ancient copper coins found today are mostly cast coins. The punchmarked copper coins are rare.[41]

Copper (Tamma) coins of the time mentioned in the texts are 'Kahavana' and 'Kagini'. Kahavana or Karsapanas were punchmarked coins in different metals. The copper karsapana weighed 80 rattis i.e. 144 grains.[42] It was prevalent in Rajagarha at the time of King Bimbasara.[43] Another copper coin mentioned is kagini (or Kakini). It was a coin of small denomination. Kautilya mentions kakini as a copper coin equal to 1/4 of a copper karsapana.[44] According to commentary on Bhat Kalpa Sutram it was a copper coin used in Daksinapatha (South).[45]

## Other Coins

Besides gold, silver and copper coins we find the prevalence of 'Kavaddage'[46] (cowries or shells) at that time. They possessed small value and as such were used for small payments. This term was also used to denote money in general.

The Nisitha Curni mentions a leather coin (cammalato)[47] issued by King Vammalata which was in use in Bhillamala (Bhinmala in District Jodhpur).[48]

## Counterfeit Coins

References in the texts reveal that counterfeit coins were also manufactured and circulated by unauthorised persons. The texts mention about false ruvages.[49] Uttaradhyāyana Sutra and many other texts refer to 'Kudakajavano' or Kuta karsapana[50] (false coins). The gold smiths (Hairanyaka) could easily detect these coins.[51]

Though some unscrupulous persons tried to manufacture and circulate false coins in those days, it seems that people could detect the counterfeit coins and as such these coins were not in general circulation.

## References

1. Upasakadasanga Sutram, Chap. I, S. 4, p. 9.
2. C.f., Idem.
3. Cf., Vyakhya Prajnapti, Part II, Chap. V.S. 106, p. 238.
4. Cf., Nisitha Sutram, Vol. III, V. 3676, p. 263.
5. Cf., Ibid., Vol. III, V. 3724, p. 274.
6. Cf., Ibid., Vol. III, pp. 340 and 394.
7. Cf., Jain, K.C. Lord Mahāvir and His Time, p. 313.
8. Cf., Nisitha Sutram, Vol. III, V. 3704, p. 270.
9. Cf., Pinda Niryukti, V. 319, p. 60.
10. Cf., Ibid
11. Cf., Jain, J.C., Agam Sahitya Mein Bhartiya Samaj, p. 111.
12. Cf., Jnatadharmakathanga Sutram, Vol. III, Chap. XV, S. 2, p. 104.
13. Cf., Ibdi., Vol. I., Chap. II, S. 2, p. 572.

14. Cf., Nisitha Sutram, Vol. I, V. 292, p. 102.
15. Cf., Ibid.
16. Cf., Ibid., Vol. III, V. 4312, p. 387.
17. Cf., Upadhyaya, V., Bharatiya Sikke, p. 6.
18. Cf., Ibid., p. 37.
19. Cf., Cunningham, A., Coins of Ancient India, p. 43.
20. Cf., Jain, K.C., op. cit., p. 306.
21. Cunningham, A., op. cit., p. 43.
22. Cf., Uttaradhyayana Sutra, Vol. II, Chap. XX, V. 42, p. 902.
23. Cf., Cunningham, A., op. cit., p. 42.
24. Cf., Ibid.
25. Cf., Upadhyaya, V., op. cit., p. 27.
26. Cf., Cunningham, A., op. cit., p. 58.
27. Cf., Jain, K.C., op. cit., p. 310.
28. Cf., Cunningham, A., op. cit., p. 60.
29. Cf., Bṛhat Kalpa Sutram, Vol. II, p. 573.
30. Cf., Nisitha Sutram, Vol. III, V. 3070, p. 111.
31. Cf., Bhandarkara, D.R., Ancient Indian Numismatics, p. 51.
32. Cf., Bṛhat Kalpa Sutram, Vol. II, p. 573.
33. Cf., Ibid., p. 573.
34. Cf., Sikdar, J.C., Studies in Bhagwati Sutra, p. 316.
35. Cf., Upadhyaya, V., op. cit., p. 27.
36. Cf., Bhandarkara, D.R. op. cit., p. 53.
37. Cf., Bṛhat Kalpa Sutram, Vol. IV, V. 3891, p. 1069.
38. Cf., Ibid.
39. Cf., Ibid., V. 3892, p. 1069.
40. Cf., Ibid., Vol. II, p. 573.
41. Cf., Cunningham, A., op. cit., p. 59.
42. Cf., Upadhyaya, V., op. cit., p. 27.
43. Cf., Upasakadassanga Sutram, appendix, p. 410.
44. Cf., Kautilya, Artha Sastra, p. 95.
45. Cf., Bṛhat Kalpa Sutram, Vol. II, p. 573.
46. Cf., Ibid.
47. Cf., Nishitha Sutram, Vol. III, 3070, p. 111.
48. Cf., Jain, K.C., Ancient Cities and Towns of Rajasthan, p. 156.
49. Cf., Avasyaka Churani, p. 550.
50. Cf., Uttaradhyayana Sutra, Vol. II, Chap. XX, V. 42. p.902.
51. Cf., Jain, J.C., op. cit., p. 119.

# Pilgrimage : A Psychological Perspective

8

*K. P. Krishna*

Religion is a universal institution. It is found in every society and culture. But the universality of religion does not mean that the form of religion is also universal. Needless to mention, religious doctrine has been a part of social, material and human development. With the increase in the complexities of the social conditions, religious practices have assumed a serious nature. Since religion has been deep-rooted in ethical and moral values, rituals and practices, totem and taboos, attitudes and beliefs, prejudices and superstitions, it has aroused much interest among social thinkers, besides those devoted to religions, religious practices and pilgrimages to holy places.

Pilgrimage is not an innate tendency, rather it is an acquired process interlinked with socialization and its certain agencies such as family, neighbourhood, caste, etc. Besides the role of child-rearing practices, stories and tales, images, values, interpersonal relationship, personal crisis, media of mass communication and moreover intrinsic and extrinsic motivations cannot be underrated. In this the principle of individual differences seems to be relevant. This is the reason why religious practices are not common to every society and culture. Some worship *Kālī* or *Durgā*, some *Śiva*, some *Hanumān* and some other Gods like *Sūrya, Viṣṇu, Mahāvīra, Buddha* etc. Similarly the method of worship or prayer differs from person to person and from place to place. People of South differ from those of North, Bengalis differ from upper and lower caste Hindus, and Muslims differ from Hindus and Jains in their ways of worship or prayer. People also differ in their practices of rituals. Although the ultimate aim of marriage is the fulfilment of *Artha, Kāma* and *Mokśa* in every religion, the rituals of marriage vary among Hindus, Bengalis, Punjabis, South Indians, Muslims, Christians, Jains, and tribals. Even in Hindu religion, it varies from caste to caste and from place to place as well.

India is a multi-religious country, comprising among its religious groups Buddhists, Christians, Hindus, Jains, Muslims, Sikhs and many more. Religion does not merely represent the faith in the unknown but it greatly affects thought and behaviour of an individual.

All religions have put great emphasis on the sacredness of certain localities and have recommended with great insistence pilgrimages to them. The four places of pilgrimage for Buddhists have been the place of the birth of Buddha (Lumbini), the place where he attained perfect enlightenment (Bodh-Gaya), the place where he delivered his first sermon (Sārnāth) and the place where he passed away into the state of *nirvāṇa* (Kushinagar). For Christians Jerusalem has been the holiest place. For Hindus the four *dhāmas* (Badrināth-Kedārnāth, Rāmeśwaram, Dwārikādhiś and Jagannāthpuri) have been the holy places of pilgrimage. Besides, large rivers, mountains and forests have always been venerated as sacred and as the abodes of Gods in India (Kane, 1953). Some of the important places of pilgrimage for Jains have been Bāhubali (Karnataka), Girinarji, Mahāvirji (Rajasthan), Champapur, Sammet Śikhar and Pāwāpuri (Bihar). Among the five incumbent practical religious duties of a Muslim, pilgrimage at least once in his life to Mecca (the birth place of the Prophet Mohammad) and Madina (the burial place of the Prophet Mohammad) is recommended.

## Meaning and Concept of Pilgrimage

The word '*tīrtha*' occurs frequently in the *Ṛgveda* and other Vedic *Samhitās.* It is often said that just as some parts of the human body (e.g. the right hand or ear) are held to be more pure than others, so some localities on the earth are held to be very holy. *Tīrthas* are held to be holy on three grounds : (a) Some wonderful natural characteristics of the locality, (b) the peculiar strikingness of some watery place, and (c) the fact that some sages resorted to them. Therefore, *tīrtha* means a locality or spot which gives rise to the accumulation of righteousness owing to its own peculiar nature without any adventitious circumstance.

The dictionary meaning of 'pilgrim' is a person who travels to a sacred place as an act of religious devotion. It is held that resort to a *tīrtha* removes the sins of the sinful and tends to the increase of merit in the case of the good and that a holy place yields fruit to men of all *varṇas* and *āśramas.*

There is no more difficult word to define than 'religion'. There are at least three reasons for this: (a) religious experience is an inward and subjective thing and it is highly individualized, (b) religion is a 'virtue word' to the average man, thus there is nothing about which people are capable of feeling more strongly than their religion, and (c) a concept of religion is influenced by the purpose of the person making the definition.

Leuba (1912) has collected fortyeight definitions of religion from various writers. He has divided his rich collection of definitions into two groups. The first group of definitions treats religion as "the recognition of a mystry pressing for interpretation." The second group of definitions adopts that religion is "a feeling of absolute dependence upon God." He adds yet a third category of definitions that treats religion as "the propitiation or conciliation of powers which are believed to direct and control the course of nature and human life."

There are a number of definitions of religion. A few of them may be cited as illustration :

"Religion is that which refers to man's faith in a power beyond himself whereby he seeks to satisfy emotional needs and gain stability of life, and which he expresses in acts of worship and service" (Galloway, 1914, p. 184).

"...religion consists of two elements, theoretical and practical, namely a belief in powers higher than man and an attempt to propitiate or please them" (Frazer, 1925, p. 50).

"Religion is the serious and social attitude of individuals or communities toward the power or powers which they conceive as having ultimate control over their interests and destinies ..." (Pratt, 1930, p. 2.).

"Religion is a felt practical relationship with what is believed in as a superhuman being or beings" (Thouless, 1936, p. 3).

"Religious sentiment is defined as a disposition, built up through experience, to respond favourably, and in certain habitual ways, to conceptual objects and principles that the individual regards of ultimate importance in his own life and as having to do with what he regards as permanent or central in the nature of things" (Allport, 1950, p. 56).

"Religion is a united system of beliefs and practices relative to sacred things, that is to say, things set apart and forbidden-beliefs and practices which unite into one single moral community called a church, and all those who adhere to them" (Durkheim, 1954, p. 47).

"Religion is the consciousness of the highest social order" (Ames, quoted by Clark, 1958, p. 20).

"A religion is a set of beliefs, practices, and institutions which men have evolved in various societies" (Parsons, quoted by Clark, 1958, p. 20).

"Religion can be most characteristically described as the inner experience of the individual when he senses a Beyond, especially as evidenced by the effect of this experience on his behaviour when he actively attempts to harmonize his life with the Beyond" (Clark, 1958, p. 22).

In the light of aforementioned definitions, it can be said that the concept of religion has attracted much attention of social scientists in general and psychologists in particular. There are many more definitions which explain religion as a psychological entity. In this context, it may be noted that being religious is different from having a religion.

## Types of Religion

Religion can be classified into several forms/types. Social scientists, particularly psychologists are not in agreement with regard to its types. However some of the representative views need to be presented.

Spinks (1963) has suggested that instead of dividing religious experiences into those which are Christian and those which are non-Christian, it would be more relevant to classify religion into *authoritarian* and *humanistic* forms. The former form demands the surrender of the individuals to some power thought of as transcending the human person (Fromm, 1951, p. 42). There are sound reasons for such an attitude. "By voluntarily submitting to a higher authority man loses his sense of personal dissatisfaction and frustration and by willingly associating himself with a Divine Power he achieves an exhilarating sense of fulfilment" (Spinks, 1963, p. 153). In contrast, the humanistic type asserts that the individual finds himself by being in loving association with his fellows. The distinction between these two types of religion refers not only to the particular beliefs which men hold collectively but also to the individual's own psychological disposition.

Allport (1960) and Allport and Ross (1967) have elaborated religious orientations into two types—'intrinsic' and 'extrinsic'. "Intrinsic religion marks the life that has interiorized the total creed of one's faith without reservation, including the commandment to love one's neighbour. A person of this sort is more intent on serving ...religion than on making it serve him" (Allport, 1960, p. 257). "Persons with this orientation find their master motive in religion. Other needs, strong as they may be, are regarded as of less ultimate significance, and they are, in so far as possible, brought into harmony with the religious beliefs and prescriptions. Having embraced a creed the individual endeavours to internalize it and follow it fully. It is in this sense that one lives one's religion" (Allport & Ross, 1967, p. 434).

On the other hand, "extrinsic religion is a self-serving, utilitarian, self-protective form of religious outlook which provides the believer with comfort and salvation at the expense of outgroups" (Allport, 1960, p. 257). "Persons with this orientation are disposed to use religion for their own ends ... Extrinsic values are always instrumental and utilitarian. Persons with this orientation may find religion useful in a variety of ways—to provide security and solace, sociability and distraction, status and self-justification. The embraced creed is lightly held or else selectively shaped to fit more primary needs. In theological term the extrinsic type turns to God, but without turning away from self" (Allport & Ross, 1967, p. 434).

Dittes (1969) in his painstaking article entitled "Psychology of Religion" has classified religion into two types—consensual and committed. The former is associated with moderately favourable attitudes and moderate attendance, correlated with conservative attitudes. The second type is associated with more intense religiosity, correlated with more liberal attitudes.

## Development of Religiousness in Individuals

Religion is not innate, it is an acquired tendency. It grows and develops in individuals through the process of socialization. Whenever a religious impulse begins to grow within a person, it has atleast the potential to mature into a more complex, integrated, and adaptive system.

Many psychological processes contribute to religious growth. Experience, parental care, images, interpersonal relationship, personal crisis, existential crisis, needs, emotions, learning, imitation, maturation, etc. are some of the psychological processes that determine the growth and development of religiousness in individuals.

Experience is a basic source of all development including religiousness. Some experiences are mediated by the sensory and perceptual systems. Others are not so clearly from outside sources. Awareness of an experience may be on an unconscious or emotional level rather than on the level of verbal consciousness. Children imitate their parents' behaviours and religious practices. They visit religious places with their parents, observe their behaviour and form a religious image. Many persons have made personal traumas like divorce, marital disharmony, family violence, etc. into avenues of religious growth (Smoke, 1976).

Walters and Bradley (1971) identified a long list of motivations that relate to religion—anger, hatred, aggression, love, achievement, conformity, dependency, acquiescence, relation to authority, quiet, fear, morality, self-concept, self-esteem, religious identity, perception of death, etc. Most of the needs lead to religious growth indirectly. Some other human drives promote growth more immediately. These drives can lead to innumerable experiences with religious implications : Visiting worship services and reading literature of different faiths, practising meditation or taking hallucinatory drugs that may produce mystical states.

Religion does not develop without the stimulation of other people. The family is principal among the social relationships that contribute to religious growth. Similarly the strong emotions roused by close interpersonal relationships partially account for their influence on religious development. Emotions in themselves are a crucial part of religion and contribute to the totality of personal faith. Trust, hope, love, friendship, compassion, bliss, etc. are among the higher emotions in many religions.

Learning, imitation and physical versus psychological maturation play an important role in developing religiousness. Learning affects and is affected by other psychological processes like perception, emotions, drives, attitudes, etc. A child cannot pray and worship until it learns to speak. In this, the role of psychosexual development and adolescence may be added. In the 'phallic stage' between ages 4 and 6 children said to form the oedipus complex. They are attracted to the parent of the opposite sex and feel hostility or envy towards the like-sexed parent. For the young boy, this is a particularly acute conflict which is finally resolved by identifying with his father and internalizing the father's prohibitions, values and religiousness. The newly activated sexual harmones, changes in primary and secondary characteristics, search for self-identity, rebellion against parental restrictions, and changing expectations from society (Knox, 1975) often lead to transformation of religious faith or lack of faith among adolescents.

## Functions of Pilgrimage

With the increase in the complexities of the social matrix, people incline to pilgrimage and religion. In his famous book 'Future of an Illusion' Freud (1927) has cited the three functions of Gods. "They must exorcize the terrors of nature, they must reconcile one to the cruelty of fate, particularly as shown in death, and they must make amends for the sufferings and privations that the communal life of culture has imposed." These can all be considered basically egocentric functions of religion.

Man is born free but everywhere he is bound in chains of DO's and DON'TS. In our society, religion starts to function when the child is in the womb and continues even after his death in some form or another. Religion is deeply linked with bodily needs, particularly sex. A number of theorists have emphasized religion as a function of sexual desires. They see sex symbols in religious myths and rituals (Allport, 1950). Sexual needs are an integral part of human life, and a comprehensive religion cannot ignore them. In Indian culture, sex symbols and different poses of sexual intercourse are artistically displayed in the temples of Khajurāho, Konārk, Puri and Sonepur. The sexual functions of earlier fertility cults and ritual prostitution are even more conspicuous than these. Certain religious traditions also provide for sexual expression and fulfilment in sanctioned relationships. *Tāntric Yoga* employs some rituals involving sexual expression.

Death is an inherent part of human conditions ; it has received considerable attention as a function of religion. (Poppleton and Pilkington 1963) have found that the British medical students, who are in frequent contact with death and dying patients, become more religious while in college. Similarly older people, among whom death is more of a present reality, become more religious than younger people (Rogers, 1976). This is more or less common to each and every religion.

Much of the insecurity of human life originates in the mind. Thus security and a number of other human needs are considered psychogenic in origin. Our most of the anxieties, insecurities, frustrations and tensions are deep-rooted in the processes of modernization, urbanization and industrialization. There is hardly any correspondence between the level of achievement and the level of aspiration. We aspire more, achieve less. Sometimes our aspiration crosses the limit of social reality. Thus it is not unnatural if a person with over aspiration develops symptoms of neurosis and psychosis, blames others for his failure, feels psychological insecurity and inclines to pilgrimage and religion. He may approach a *tāntric, astrologer* or *priest* for his advice to fulfil his aspiration. In the same process he may perform *pūjā, pāṭha or kathā,* he may wear astrological stones or he may start visiting temples regularly and proceed on journey to religious places. Although this practice is more or less common to every field, such as education, business, service, cultivation and so on, it is more applicable to politics. Political men directly or indirectly follow the instructions of a *tāntric,* astrologer or *yogi* to fulfil their long-cherished desires of having power and status.

Maslow (1954) presents a hierarchy of needs (such as esteem, self-actualization, self-transcendence) which are expressed in intrinsic and extrinsic religious practices. Religion has also cognitive and individualizing functions. Scientific accounts of the nature and causes of earthquakes, famine, volcanic eruptions, floods, etc. do not provide satisfactory answers. Finding no solution, individuals surrender themselves to God and His Supreme Power. This process provides them mental peace and pursues them for creative works. This is the reason why some businessmen, service holders, cultivators, social reformers, educationists and politicians help the victims of natural calamities and provide them relief. Efforts are also made by some persons to help the weaker sections of society. The underlying motive may be to please the Supreme Power and to purify the soul.

Some people in our society are very much afraid of going to hell after death as heard from the religious *gurus* and read in religious books. They unconsciously help the humanity, although they are corrupt and disreputed. Rehabilitation of victims of floods, earthquakes, handicapped and eradication of social evils, etc. are always considered to be a pious work in every religion. Therefore corrupt businessmen and even politicians are deeply involved in it. Establishment of *dharmśālās,* temples and religious institutions are also considered to be the persuasion of religiousness. Many a time it is heard that a person in power has no issue. On the advice of his *Dharmaguru,* he constructed or renovated a temple; and he is blessed with a son. Thus despite present and future advances of science and technology, many meaningful questions await religious insights.

Several theorists have suggested that religious feelings and behaviours precede religious thoughts. Sometimes religious thinking serves to explain to people the meaning of their feelings or acts.

Religious beliefs may be individualized in two contrasting ways. Some people hold a religion quite casually. They are inclined to accept just the parts of their religious systems that are convenient and helpful at the moment; this is a relatively egocentric use of religion. On the other hand, some people have temperaments and experiences that make significant portions of their given religious package unacceptable. Yet they labour to develop their own most consistent, well-integrated, and intellectually defensible religious solutions. The development of their religion is obviously a self-actualizing process. Thus people can handle their religious cognitions in either egocentric or growth ways.

Religion has also its social functions. It promotes the integrity of society, conformity and affiliation. Some sociologists like Durkheim (1915), Bellah (1968), Tanenbaum (1975) and several others have emphasized the function religion plays in forging and preserving a social order. It functions variously in the social and cultural areas of human life. The psychological tendency to conform serves the interests of religion. Needless to mention, conformity helps people to bind together in a common identity. Religion offers many people an opportunity for social contact, quite apart from the inherently religious purposes of church, temples, mosque or *Gurudwārā.* For many Hindus, visiting

*Hanumān, Kālī, Durgā or Śiva* temples before and after service hours and other specific social activities are inseparable parts of the religious life. People establish such temples near railway station, bus stand and in the vicinity of crowded market so that willing persons may come easily and worship. This may be considered as gregariousness, the herd instinct, just wanting to be with other people.

Why do people go to pilgrimage at distant religious places ? The answer may be sought in the unconscious motivation. Man is very much perturbed in the present modern complex society, he wants some change. Megalpolis, metropolis and cities cannot satisfy his instincts, divert his thoughts and reduce his mental agonies and frustrations. Therefore he intends to visit calm and quiet places located in the lap of nature. Keeping this psychology in view, most of the religious places and *tīrthās* centre around the holy rivers, seas, mountains/hills and forests. Thus visit to these places serves three purposes—change in routined life, diversion of thoughts, and worship of Gods/Goddesses and purification of soul.

In ancient time pilgrimage serves many purposes of the community as well as of the pilgrims themselves. Though ancient India was divided into many kingdoms and the Indian people followed several cults and sub-cults, pilgrimage tended to foster the Indian ideology, culture, moral and religious values as well. Though the Hindu community was mostly caste-ridden and broken-up into numerous castes and suffered from caste exclusiveness, pilgrimage tended to level up all persons by bringing them together to the same holy rivers or shrines.

The traditions associated with holy places, the discipline through which the pilgrims passed, interaction with holy and philosophic men, and the whole atmosphere/environment present at *tīrthas* made it easy for pilgrims to remain at a high spiritual level and inculcated in them a mood of reverence that lasted long even after they returned from the pilgrimage.

Pilgrimage supplies the much needed stimulus to draw ordinary men away from selfish pursuits and to make them think of the higher and enduring moral and spiritual values. These benefits and the belief that a holy place is the abode of some divinity motivate ancient Dharmaśāstra writers lay more emphasis on visits to *tīrthas*. Needless to mention, the *dharma* common to all men comprises such elements as forbearance, truthfulness, restraint of the mind, cleanliness, charity, control of the senses, *ahiṃsā*, obedience to elders, visiting holy places, compassion, straightforwardness, freedom from avarice, honouring Gods and *brāhmaṇas*, and freedom from jealousy.

To conclude, pilgrimage and religion serve many purposes. Sometimes suppressed wishes which are socially undesirable and one cannot dare express them before a human being can easily be expressed before the Gods during pilgrimage. After this the person feels relief and mental peace. Thus pilgrimage has also Cathartic function. In this way, pilgrimage has mainly biological, cognitive, egocentric, moral, spiritual, social and psychological functions. These functions vary from society to society as well as from culture to culture. As psychological insecurity, tension, anxiety, frustration, violence, etc. will increase in society, human beings, finding no way out, will incline to religion and devote some time in visiting *tīrthas* for religious practices.

## References

Allport, G.W. (1950), *The individual and his religion*. New York : Macmillan.

Allport, G.W. (1960), *Personality and social encounter*. Boston : Beacon Press.

Allport, G.W. & Ross, J.M. (1967), Personal religious orientation and prejudice. *Journal of Personality and Social Psychology, 5*, 432–443.

Bellah, R.N. (1968), Civil religion in America. In William G. McLoughlin & Robert N. Bellah (Eds.) *Religion in America*. Boston : Beacon Press.

Clark, W.H. (1958), *The psychology of religion*. New York : Macmillan.

Dittes, J.E. (1969), Psychology of religion. In Gardner Lindzey & E. Aronson (Eds) *The handbook of social psychology*, Vol. 5, Reading M.A.: Addison-Wesley, pp. 602–659.

Durkheim, Emile (1915), *The elementary forms of the religious life*. (Trans. J.W. Swain). New York : Free Press.

Durkheim, Emile (1954), *The elementary forms of religious life*. London : Allen & Unwin.

Frazer, James G. (1935), *The golden bough* (Abridged ed). New York : Macmillan.

Freud, S. (1927), *The future of an illusion.* Translated by W.D. Robson-Scott. London : The Hogarth Press, 1962.

Fromm, Erich (1951), *Psychoanalysis and religion.* London : Victor Gollance.

Galloway, G. (1914), *The philosophy of religion.* Edinburgh : T. & T. Clark.

Kane, P.V. (1953), *History of Dharmasastra,* Vol. 4, Pune : Bhandarkar Oriental Research Institute.

Knox, Ian (1975), Religion and the expectations of modern society towards the adolescent. *Religious Education,* 70, 649–660.

Leuba, J.H. (1912), *A psychological study of religion.* New York : Macmillan.

Maslow, A.H. (1954), *Motivation and personality.* New York : Harper & Row.

Poppleton, P.K. & Pilkington, G.W. (1963), The measurement of religious attitudes in a University Population. *British Journal of Social and Clinical Psychology, 2,* 20–36.

Pratt, J.B. (1930), *The religious consciousness.* London : Macmillan.

Rogers, Tommy (1976), Manifestations of religiosity and the aging process. *Religious Education, 71,* 405–415.

Smoke, Jim (1976), *Growing through divorce.* Irvine Ca : Harvest House.

Spinks, G.S. (1963) *Psychology and religion : An introduction to contemporary views.* London : Methuen & Co. Ltd.

Tanenbaum, M.H. (1975), Civil religion : Unifying force or idolatry. *Religious Education, 70,* 469–473.

Thouless, R.H. (1936), *An introduction to the psychology of religion.* London: Cambridge University Press.

Walters, A. & Bradley, R. (1971), Motivation and religious behaviour. In Meton P. Strommen (Ed.) *Research on religious development : A comprehensive handbook.* New York : Howthorn, pp. 599–651.

# Jainism in Magadh Region

**9**

*M. K. Sharan*

Magadh was the main centre of Mahāveer's activities. And major valuable part of his ascetic life was spent at Rājagṛh and its vicinity. He breathed his last at Pāvāpuri near the old Magadhan capital. His eleven disciples led a successful life in Magadh. They all devoted their whole lives in Magadh for the propagation of the faith. According to Jinacharya we know that Gautam Gandhara became the spiritual leader of the Jains in the year 527 B.C.[1] He himself attained salvation after twelve years and then was succeeded by Sudharmacharya.[2] He also led the *Saṁgha* for twelve years. After him the leadership of the *Saṁgha* went to Jambusvami[3] who was the spiritual head for thirty-eight years. After these three, Nande, Nandimitra, Aparajita, Govardhana and Bhadrabāhu[4] became leaders in succession and the total period of their leadership covers one hundred years. All these Jain *āchāryas* were born in the pious land of Magadh and its neighbourhood though the sphere of their religious activities extended widely beyond the region. Gautam Gandhara attained salvation at Gunaya in Nawada district. Likewise the Parsvanath hill is credited to have been the place of salvation of many other Jain spiritual leaders. After these, eleven *arhats* namely Viśhākhadatta, Proshthila, Chatriya, Jaya, Nāga, Siddhārtha, Sthitisen, Vijaya Buddhila, Gangadeva and Sudharma became the possessors of the ten *pūrvajñāna.* They led the Jain *Saṁgha* for 183 years in all. After them Nakshatra, Javanapala Pandu, Dhruvasena and *Kamsa* became *āchāryas* of the eleven *Angajñana.*[6] The period of their leadership covers 220 years. These religious leaders were later followed by the four *āchāryas* who had but a partial knowledge of the *Aṅga* and *Pūrva* wisdoms.[7] Thus the tradition of Jain *āchāryas* continued from 327 B.C. to 56 A.D. Though they all travelled throughout India for preaching and propagating the Doctrine, Magadh was the main centre of their spiritual exercises.[8]

Both Jain and Buddhist traditions claim that during Bimbisāra's and Ajātaśatru's reign masters of both the sects flourished. But by all indications the initial success of the Jains was by far greater. The *Uttaradhyavana Sūtra*[9] describes how Bimbisāra met Mahāveer, a lion among *anagara* monks at Mandikushi chaitya along with his queens and a troop of servants and relatives. Here the Magadhan king adopted Jainism with great devotion and fan-fare. The credit of this conversion may perhaps go to his Lichchhavi queen Chellana. Bimbisāra's consistency in spiritual allegiance is underlined by the fact that much later when the country was tormented by a violent snow-storm he visited Mahāveer with Chellana.[10]

Ajātaśatru was probably a Jain atleast in his early days. Jain texts speak highly of his devotion to the doctrine. The Jain sectarian lore does not hold him guilty of particide, which is a strong point to the spiritual loyalty of the king. He is said to be paying regular visits to Nataputta in company of his queens and servants. He met the *Tirthaṅkara* even beyond the frontiers of his kingdom.[11] In the *Aupatika Sutta,*[12] we find him telling Mahāveer himself that the latter had preached the true religion and his message of renunciation and non-violence illuminated the path of religion.

The Jain ascendancy in the royal household of Magadh continued with same vigour after Ajātaśatru. His śuccessor Udaya was also a patron of the faith like his father. His serious interest in the Jain *Saṁgha* is evident from the sad fact that he was killed by a prince while in the attires of a monk. From the Hāthiguṁpha inscription of king Khāravela we know that the first Nanda king had carried away the image of Ādi Jina from the Kalinga capital, which establishes that Jainism found favour with the Nandas also. Significantly enough, Jain texts have said nothing against any Nanda except the first one. The ministers of Nanda kings were also Jains. One such minister was Kālāsoka who was initially reluctant to join the post. It is said that the grand plan of destroying all contemporary Kshatriya dynasties was prepared with his help. From his family were recruited the ministers of the later Nandas.[13] The ninth minister was Sakatala who had two sons, Sthulabhadra and Śravaka. After the demise of Sakatala, Sthulabhadra was offered the post but he declined and became a Jain recluse by receiving sermon from the Sixth *Jina.*[14] The association of *Nandas* with Jains is further confirmed by the *Mudrārākśasa* reference which states that Chanakya chose a Jain as his chief spy for knowing the secrets of the Nandas. From the Avassaya tradition,[15] we know that Chānakya was himself the son of a Jain layman.

Towards the close of the *Nanda* rule the Jain *Saṁgha* came to be led by two *arhats,* namely Sambhutivijaya and Bhadrabāhu. After the passing away of the former in the reign of Chandragupta Maurya his disciple Sthūlabhadra succeeded to the monastic presidentship. Exactly at the same time Magadh came in the grip of a twelve year famine. To save the Saṁgha, Bhadrabāhu led it to the South and settled at Śravanabelagola. As the legends go the Magadhan Emperor Chandragupta also remounced the world of power and accompanied the *Saṁgha* as a monk. He himself had joined Bhadrabāhu's march to the South as his disciple. A cave is dedicated to him and the hill on which it exists is known as Chandragiri after him. When the famine was over, the *Saṁgha* returned back to Magadh but Bhadrabāhu handed over his position to Sthūlabhadra and went away to Nepal. This was an epoch of internal revolution in the Jain synod. The monks who returned from the South were surprised to see the monks who had stayed back in Magadh during the famine. They held the white-robed monks guilty of deviation from the path of the *vinaya,* by shunning *achelakadharma* and declared them heretics. Because the old *Aṅgās* had by then been lost there were endless debates between the two groups of monks and the rift kept widening. Finally the white robed monks decided to convoke a congregation at Pātaliputra in order to canonise the Doctrine, but the monks who had returned from Śravanbelagola refused to attend it. It so happened that the old sectarian literature consisting of eleven *Angas* composed by *Gandharva* and fourteen *pūrvas* told by Mahāveer was known by heart only to Bhadrabāhu. When Sthulabhadra met him in Nepal for reconstructing it Bhadrabāhu permitted preaching of only first ten *pūrvas*. Thus the Pātaliputra congregation was to only partially restore the sectarian literature which was now called *Siddhānta*. It also included some new texts and was to be the basis of the *Śvetāmbara Āgama*. The monks of Bhadrabāhu's erstwhile group considered themselves representatives of the older and purer *Saṁgha* and came to be known as *Digambaras*. In their view the old literature had altogether been lost for ever.

Under Aśoka—the third king of the Mauryan dynasty Buddhism was in for grand revival. Already weakened by the rift, the Jain *Saṁgha* had now lost the royal patronage. It, therefore, gradually began losing its place of eminence in the east and now tended to shift its moorings westwards. Nevertheless, Jainism was still a living force in Magadh under Aśoka. He had counted it as an important *pāshanda* of the time. As a matter of fact also grandson *Samprati* is considered to be the greatest royal patron of Jainism. But his capital was at Ujjain. According to Hemachandra, Samprati devoted himself to Jain mission work among the Āndhras and Dramilas in South India which are both said to be under his command.[16]

The position of Jainism in the Shung age is not clear from literary accounts. But in all probabilities it continued to command recognizable following during this period. In the course of excavation at the Maniyāra Math site at Rajagṛha an inscribed image of Pārshvanāth with seven hooded disc has been obtained. This artistically unique image has been dated by Dr. K.P. Jayaswal in the 1st century A.D.

## The Classical Age and After

It is not easy to reconstruct the history of Jainism during the Gupta period due to paucity of literary as well as epigraphic sources. The fulcrum of its strength had by now decidedly shifted to western India where, at Mathura and Valabhi sectarian councils were convened in the 4th-5th century A.D. Rightly do most scholars believe that the Jain religion had lost much of its influence in Magadh, the country of its origin under the Gupta rulers.[17]

The picture was not entirely dismal as is proved by some archaeological findings as well as literary references. There is no doubt that the Jains continued to flourish in the Rajagṛha area. R.P. Chandra refers to a black basalt image of Nemināth, the 22nd *Tirthaṅkara* fixed on the wall of the ruined temple on the Vaibhara hill.[18] This image carries a mutilated inscription bearing the legend "*(Ma)hārāja (dhi) rā (ja) Śrī Chandra*" in early Gupta characters. Obviously this image belongs to the reign of Chandragupta II. There are also three standing *Tirthaṅkara* images in the same shrine which have also been assigned to the Gupta age.[19] On the same hill there stands in *Khaḍgāsana* a fine figure of Mahāveer with an indistinct inscription of about the fifth century A.D. on its pedestal.[20] On the basis of an inscription of the 3rd 4th century A.D., on the outer wall, and relief representation of six *Tīrthaṅkara* figures on the Southern wall of the Western and Eastern Sonabhadra caves respectively, Kuraishi and Ghosh claim a Jain origin for the caves.[21] It must however, be noted that Alexander Cunningham and Beglar had regarded them as the caves of Buddha and Ananda.

In the post-Gupta time Magadh's pristine glory in the Jain world was not all lost. Jain preachers from all over the country visited the country not only to preach their religion but also to indulge in the pious exercise of sightseeing which was called "the perusal of the Janapada." The ascetics felt a sense of purity by this Janapada-darśana. They stayed long and acquired knowledge of several languages during their sojourn. In course of their stay the Jain saints used to visit the places of birth, initiation and enlightenment of the *Tīrthaṅkaras*.[22] One of such ascetics was Saṅghadāsa Muni who belongs to the sixth century A.D. In his treatise, Vasudeva Muni, he has many good things to say about the Magadh Janapada. He writes that the region was full of shady trees rich with flowers and fruits. Lotus and lily flowers adorned its ponds and tanks. Travellers had to fare no difficulty in that Janapada to its affluence Rajagriha was fortified with moats and walls within which the *Śramaṇas* and *Brāhmaṇas* lived in harmony. There was a temple called Gunasilalaya where the religious teachers stayed. In the sixth century A.D. again, a saint named Vimala Suri also made a pilgrimage to the Magadh Janapada and his treatise '*paumachariyaṁ*', a *Prakrita* work indicates that the condition of Jainism in the Magadh of that time was quite satisfactory.

How far the Jainism of sixth century A.D., Magadh had been contaminated by folk cults is reflected in the description of some *Chaityas* furnished by the commentaries and churnis of the time. Jain ascetics used to stay and worship in such shrines. Mention is made of the Vyantaravatana (having images of the *Vyantaras*) *Chaitya* of Amalakaopa and Dvipalasa. These *Yaksh* temples were situated on the outskirts of Rajagṛha. Even Jain *Śrāvakas* worshipped in these temples to acquire worldly accomplishments. Bhadrā, the wife of Dhanya Sārthavāha worshipped in these temples with food, drink etc on the eighth, fourteenth and fifteenth days of the Lunar month. Eventually her desire for a son was granted. Another grand and famous yaksha temple was the ancient Pūrvabhadra *chaitya* where also Jain ascetics stayed.

From Hiuen tSang's accounts we know that Rajagṛha continued to be a favourite resort for the Jain mendicants. The vipula mountain of the old Magadh capital was a seat of such ascetics during the visit of the Chinese traveller. He laments that on the spot, where Buddha once preached, many *Digaṁbaras* now lodged and practised austerities incessantly.[23] This hill has been identified with the Vaibhāra hill.[24] Hiuen tSang's information is well corroborated by the *Padmācharita* in which Āchārya Ravisena gives the account of Jainism under Harśa. From it we gather that the religion was in a flourishing condition in Magadh and many other parts of Bihar. Numerous temples of *Tīrthaṅkaras* were being built and the teachers were always on the move in the sacred places to propagate the Doctrine. It is interesting to note that various images of *Ādināth* with head locks found in some of the Jain temples at Gaya which belong to the sixth-seventh century A.D. have forms corresponding to the guidelines contained in the *Padmapurāṇa* of the same Ravisena.

It is, however, difficult to ascertain whether the Āchārya based his guidelines on the sculptural varieties of his time or the case was just reverse. That sculptors of this period were much busy with Jain images is further confirmed by broken icons found on the various hill of Rajagṛha.

The flourishing condition of Jainism in the eighth century is known from both literary and archaeological sources. In the course of enumerating the principles of the Doctrine Āchārya Jñanasena hints at the popularity of Jainism in the Magadh of his time. Āchārya Haribhadra of the same century has also referred to Kusumpura or Pātaliputra in the work *Samaraicha Kaha*. According to his description rich men of Magadh were constructing Jain temples in those days. The veracity of his statement is proved by the fact that same of the broken images of *Rajagṛha* hills are dated in the eighth century A.D.

A lot of information has come to light regarding the condition of Jainism in the ninth-tenth century A.D. Magadh from the excavations at the site of *Koluha* hill summit in Chatra district. A temple of *Pārshvanāth* has been discovered by a pond there. A little further there lies a mound the upper part of which is levelled with a big hole identified as a *Yajña Kunda*. The inscriptions unearthed here have not yet been fully deciphered. But the occurrence of a word 'Jaunasen' in one of them has led some to the presumption that here was the courtyard of Jinasen (9th century A.D.).[25] From the *Bṛhatakosha* of Harisen of the tenth century A.D., we learn that Jainism was an important sect in Magadh in his time. From the legend of Jinadatta and Mitrasre it appears that the Doctrine was adhered to mostly by people of the middle class such as caravan leaders, architects, potters and gentries.[26] The Baragaon Jain temple epigraph of the reign of Rajyapāla, the Pāla dynasty of the first half of the tenth century A.D., bears testimony to this fact by recording pilgrimage to the site of a trader called Sri Vaidyanāth, son of one Manoratha. The *Bṛhatakathā* also hints at ill will prevailing between Jains and Buddhists. The story of Padmaśri, the daughter of Rishabhadatta, a Jain teacher of Rajagṛha, who was tortured by her Buddhist father-in-law can be constructed as a proof of the declining influence of Jainism in Magadh.

In the succeeding centuries Jain works began to take less and less notice of the most parts of Bihar. But because of its special sanctity *Rajagṛha* continued to win the admiration of Jain writers. Poet Arhaddās placed between the last quarter of the twelfth century and the first quarter of the thirteenth century and the first quarter of the thirteenth century A.D., has eulogize the ancient Magadh capital in his poetic work *Muni Subrata Kāvya.* Jinaprabhu Suri, who belongs to the first quarter of the thirteenth century A.D. counts Rajagṛha and Pātaliputra along with Mithilā and Champāpura as places of Jain pilgrimage. Archaeological findings testify to the fact that Jain temples continued to be constructed in this period. At Gunaya, which is hallowed by the memory of Gautama Gandhara, an image of Vasupujya installed in 1211 A.D., has been discovered.[28] There is another image of the same date of Kunthunāth found on an altar. The altar is new but the numerous images installed are certainly medieval. In the Jalamandira temple images of Vasipujya and Mahāveer bearing *Śvetāṁbara* emblems have been discovered. The twenty four foot prints representing the twenty four *Tīrthaṅkaras* also bear *Śvetāmbara* emblems. The foot prints are not very old but other accessories of the temple seem to be certainly medieval.

## References

1. Maity, P., Studies in Ancient India, Calcutta, 1969, p. 71.
2. Mehta, M.L., Jaina philosophy, Varanasi, 1971, p. 26.
3. Muni, Shri Nagrajji, The Contemporaneity and the Chronology of Mahavira and Buddha, New Delhi, 1970, p. 25.
4. Tilopavannathi, 4/1476.
5. Ibid. 4/1485-88.
6. Gokhale, B.K. and others, Ancient Indian History and Culture, Bombay, 1970, p. 135.
7. Lunia, B.N., Evolution of Indian Culture, Agra, 1970, p. 122.
8. Tilopavannathi, 4/1489-91.
9. Majumdar, R.C. (edited), The Age of Imperial Unity, Bombay, 1968, p. 411 ff.

10. Hemachandra, Triṣaṣti Śalākhā, 106, 10-11
11. 12. 27. 30
12. 30
13. Avasyaka Sutra, pp. 691-693.
14. Tilopavannathi, 4/1476
15. Ibid.
16. Jacobi, Sathaviravali, 2nd edition, p. ix.
17. Dịwakar, R.R., (1959), Bihar through the Ages, Patna, p. 283.
18. ASIAR, 1925-26, p. 125.
19. Majumdar, B.P. (1974), Comprehensive History of Bihar, pt II, Patna, p. 136.
20. Kuraishi, M.H. (1951), and Ghosh, A., Rajgir, Patna, p. 18.
21. Ibid.
22. Motichanda, Jain Siddharta Bhaskara, XIX, 2.
23. Watters on Yanchwang, Vol II, p. 154.
24. Law, B.C., Rajagṛha in Ancient Literature, p. 6.
25. Ray Choudhary, P.C., Jainism in Bihar, p. 40.
26. Shastri, N.C., Compreshensive History of Bihar, Vol I, Pt. I, 1974, p. 485.
27. I. 22-54.
28. Brahmacharini Pandit Chandra Bai Abhinandana Grantha, p. 125.

# Mahāveer's Path of Sādhanā

**10**

*V. R. Agrawal*

Mahāveer's *sādhanā* was internal *sādhanā*. During the long period of about 2500 years much has been written about him, but the internal form of his *sādhanā* is quite scanty, though its analysis also like that of his auspicious preaching is highly essential. Mahāveer was externally not so much as he was internally. So his internal life is most important. But unfortunately on this viewpoint ancient writers are generally silent. Notwithstanding, on the basis of the various events of the period of his *sādhanā* we can even today some what hypothesize regarding the path of his internal *sādhanā*.

The external form of his *sādhanā* is *āchāra* (conduct). He renounced home after being free from *parigraha* both internally, as well as externally. He possessed nothing in the name of wealth; no means even for the fulfilment of the basic needs of life. He, a prince surrounded by thousands of servants, self initiated proceeded all alone towards lovely forests where death lurked at every step; even then he neither kept a single servant to serve him, nor any weapon for his protection, nor any scripture for study. At the time of renunciation he possessed only a single price of cloth which too, he later on doled out. This was Mahāveer's perfect state of non-possession, amply described in biographical works.

Mahāveer's path of penance was fully independent. The contemporary paths of *sādhanā* as prevailed in the society, were not acceptable to him. His path of *sādhanā* was internal and spontaneous. Experiences and attainments of the previous day opened the path of the following day so his long period of penance did not belong to any particular path. Externally his *sādhanā* underwent sufficient changes. This is why many of his actions do not exactly tally with the present code of conduct.

Non-attachment is the life-blood of his *sādhanā*. The external form of his *sādhanā* is secondary because it is not eternal; in his own words it is not the main current of his *sādhanā*. The life-blood of his *sādhanā* is complete non-attachment which is the real path of his *sādhanā*. No doubt for the accomplishment of complete non-attachment something more is prescribed and practised as an equipment but actually that 'more' is not actually more. On delving deep we see that it too, is nothing except nourisher and protector of the true non-attachment.

True non-attachment in itself is both *sādhanā* and *siddhi*. It forms Mahāveera's whole philosophy of life and his path of *sādhanā* . It alone is virtually the starting as well as the last point of his *sādhanā*. The only difference is that of its completeness or incompleteness. Successive stages of development of non-attachment are *sādhanā* and never decaying. Completeness is *siddhi,* the final point of *sādhanā*.

Attachment and malice are the cloud covering the sun of consciousness. Desire is attachment and malice is hatred. From time immemorial the soul has been covered by these screens. Bandage of the soul is nothing else except this. Mahāveer himself says, "Attachment and malice, these two alone, constitute the bondage. As the thousand-rayed sun gets screened by the cloud, so is the multi-rayed soul screened by attachment and malice. The sun itself creates the cloud and itself destroys it. The sun removes the cloud while the soul itself withdraws. It is said that Mahāveer removed the screen, broke the fetters. This simply means that he turned his *bhāva* from outward towards inward; his *bhāva* leaving the form of *vibhāva* adopted that of *svabhāva* and thus he was freed from the bondage. *Vibhāva* is bondage and *svabhāva* is liberation. Attachment and malice are nothing but state of duality (vikalpa). When there is duality then alone attachment and malice exist. Fetters lie in duality. When one withdraws the second automatically goes. When the soul gets rid of duality then attachment and malice based on it not only withdraw but become non-existent. In the face of parity (samatā) disparity (visamatā) cannot exist.

The infinite soul has neither screens nor fetters. All these are super imposed. Mahāveer did not accept the long-accepted bondage and he became free from attachment. Meditation is the unfailing means of freedom from bondage. It is an internal process of awakening the divinity lying dormant within us. Meditation is the spiritual art of reviving the memory of the forgotten 'self'.

The aggregate of our life is highly complicated and crowded. It has many layers. The most corpulent layer is this visible body. Then there are sense organs, mind and the mental perversions. Like the spring of water buried beneath so many layers, the pure consciousness also is lying buried beneath those layers. Body is the uppermost layer, sense organs, form the lower layer and the mind forms the lowest layer. Body is nothing but conglomeration of bones, flesh, marrow, urine, clay and water. Sense organs are subtler than the body. But they have their access upto the experience of only physical thing such as form, taste and smell etc. Mind forms the most complicated layer. It is such a bubble of resolve and uncertainty as keeps the consciousness of man badly entangled. Attachment and malice and their subtle manifestation in the forms of perversions, excitement, hatred, envy and ego etc. are first born in the internal mind. Later on, from there, through the body and the sense organs, they manifest themselves in good forms.

The layers of body and sense organs are not much harmful, virtually not harmful at all. From the point of view of *sādhanā* it is not essential to break these layers. In the accomplishment of non-attachment neither the body nor the sense organs create any hurdle. Attachment and malice do not exist in the body. Their centre is neither body nor sense organs; it is mind. Even mind by itself does not muddle. As subduing body and the sense organs is not *sādhanā* so subduing the mind also is not *sādhanā*. Mind in itself is not bad, bad are the mental perversions. *Sādhanā* is nothing but breaking the layers of perversions, cleaning the dirt of the consciousness. In the hue and cry of the crowd of perversions the original voice of consciousness is merged. Aim of *sādhanā* is to make this voice audible by calming down the hue and cry of the crowd. Till there is crowd the hue and cry shall continue and the voice of the consciousness shall remain submerged in it. So it is essential to disperse the crowd itself.

Attachment and malice are the seeds of innumerable and infinite perversions such as lust, anger, arrogance, greed and delusion etc. *Sādhanā* is the spontaneous attainment of consciousness in the direction of freeing itself from attachment and malice. When the consciousness, being free reaches its pure and original form and firmly establishes itself in its pure state, then it becomes supreme consciousness, the Supreme Principle. The spiritual process of attaining this Supreme Soul is itself the *sādhanā* that Mahāveer accepts.

Meaning of *sādhanā* is freedom from perversions and realisation of the pure and conscious soul lying concealed within us. When we look at our old and new religious traditions, we find that some are following the path of suppression (damana). There are many sadhaks who severely torture their bodies. In biting cold they remain naked and in terrible heat cover their body with blankets. During the coldest months of *Pausa* and *Māgha* remain standing in water throughout the night; in the mid-day heat of the months of *Vaiśākha* and *Jyeṣtha* sit surrounded by fire burning on all the four sides, some lie on thorns, some spend years in standing posture and even pass faceas and urine like animals; some chew dry grass and leaves and some eat moss produced on the surface of water; some even damage their eyes and ears and became blind and deaf, some in extreme enthusiasm to get freedom from perversion, go to the extent of cutting off their penis.

In the age of Mahāveer also there were thousands of such *sādhakās.* They have been frequently mentioned in Jain as well as in Vedic literature. Among the experiments being performed by them to bring the internal propensities to the zero point these are the experiments of suppression (damana). Suppression is the malignant (tāmasa) experiment to control the inauspicious propensities arising within us. In such experiments there is nothing except indiscreet obstinacy to check momentarily the activities of the body and the sense organs. The serpent is sitting inside and hissing and the people with their eyes closed are striking the snake's hole. Pain is elsewhere and medicine is applied somewhere else. Violence, falsehood, hatred, enmity, greed and infatuation are neither the perversions of body nor of the sense-organs. It is needless to torture these innocent and poor life long companions; they in no way damage us.

It is right that the *sādhaka* as a precautionary measure keeps himself vigilant in respect of body and sense organs and does not leave them unrestrained. In the initial stage, to some extent, control over them is essential. But all this should take place only to a particular limit, in the pure light of discretion. It should not cross the limit of propriety and *sādhanā,* only adopt the perverted form of bodily torture. Mahāveer's *sādhanā* is not that of suppression. It is true that Mahāveer lived naked, observed severe penances and practised *sādhanā* mostly in lovely wild tracts away from human population but for him all this was quite natural, was spontaneous not perforce imposed from outside. His external conduct lay within the limit of his own power and was justified. Virtually this was not *sādhanā* itself but a process to prepare a good environment for it. In his post-*sādhanā* period, he names it as external penance. When we treat anything as external its intrinsic value becomes obvious in our eyes. This is why adopted external practices at the proper time but with out being stuck to them. When needed he effected proper changes in them, one who sticks, can never do so.

Thus Mahāveer's *sādhanā* was not that of suppression. Virtually suppression is not *sādhanā* at all. By indiscreet and blind control propensities cannot be purified. They may utmost be a means of getting public cheers but not the *sādhanā* that arouses our innerself.

The basis of suppression is imprudence and ignorance. In it there is no consideration of proper or improper but there exists only ego-based obstinacy. A *sādhaka* of suppression mostly lays stress on the traditional social regulations and regards them as the final aim of *sādhanā.* Thus such a *sādhaka* easily attains the popularity of being religious and spiritual. Then he begins to adopt other tactics to widen his circle. To prove that he is number one and others are number two or three or nowhere evolves new methods of difficult and miraculous religious rites. And then falling in the trap of attainments and popularity he stands nowhere.

In the world of religion there exists an ugly atmosphere of mutual slander and criticism. The reason is that the hunger for fame in such a *sādhaka* is so intense that to satisfy it he goes mad; tries to pull others, down from the throne of fame and install him on it. So to maintain the already attained popularity and to attain further popularity he on one hand adopts the path of such severest miraculous religious rites as astonish the common people and on the other hand for other *sādhakas* and religious persons create an atmosphere of slander.

Suppression which claims to check inauspicious propensities is itself inauspicious. What in itself is inauspicious but outwardly puts on the garb of suspiciousness is virtually not auspicious and so cannot remove inauspiciousness. None can render black coal white even by washing it in milk. Rāvana cannot become Rāma by dressing him as Ram. In the same way inauspicious and perverted propensities cannot be made auspicious by life-less controls in the form of physical tortures. Under the cover of outwardly attractive masks proclaimed as restraint, there exists the ugliness of perversions. An attractive mask may utmost keep the ugliness hidden, but cannot wipe it out. So suppression can not drive out the propensities, it only falsely poses or pretends to do so.

Many a time it so happens that the perversions are not actually destroyed but there is only illusion of their being destroyed and this illusion deceives the *sādhaka* at the last moment. A serpent concealed under snow appears to be dead but as soon as it gets heat, it starts hissing. Suppression hides the propensities for a few moment, even mitigates them but nothing more. The *sādhaka* thinking that he has got success sits relaxed. But this path is full of danger, so is not the right path of *sādhanā*.

Contrary to the path of suppression there is another path which allows the propensity free play. The followers of this path say, as soon as a propensity arises in the mind, it should be satisfied at all costs. Not suppressed but satisfied propensities render the mind light and thus by leading a free and a licentious life the path of the attainment of the goal and spiritual piety is smoothed. But this path also is not worth following. Propensities cannot be satisfied by fulfilment. If we pour ghee into the fire, it blazes up; it is not extinguished. Near the current of a river when people dig a pit in the sand, it gradually gets filled with water. When water is thrown off they go empty but this emptiness is not permanent. They do not dry forever. This is also true in the context of propensities. By satisfying them we think that we have got rid of them, but it is not so. For sometime appearance of riddance, momentary solution, is got but it is not permanent and real. As by suppression only satisfying propensities are not destroyed. So a true follower of Mahāveer neither suppresses nor satisfies propensities.

Mahāveer's path of *sādhanā* is unique and different from both of these paths. His path is that of discretion and consciousness. It follows the middle path lying between retirement and attachment. External prescriptive and prohibitive rules are acceptable to him only to a certain extent. But his main path of *sādhanā* is not external but internal. Neither suppression nor fulfilment of propensities but their corrosion (*kṣapaṇa*) was his ideal. In the scriptural language, it is called path of corrosion (*kṣāyi kamārga*). In this path of *sādhanā* the seeds of the propensities are traced out and then their bases are ascertained. To bring them to zero point pure scientific spiritual method is applied. Thus Mahāveer's path of *sādhanā* was the path of corrosion which uproots the propensities and perversions of life and the *sādhaka* reaches the summit of development of his consciousness.

Meditation forms the main basis of the *sādhanā* of non-attachment. He neither recommends suppression nor fulfilment of propensities but their corrosion. So it is *sādhanā* of corrosion and its main basis is meditation. This virtually formed the internal path of Mahāveer's *sādhanā.* Through this path he reveals his internal infinite divine dignity and achieves the pure spiritual existence. The meaning itself of meditation is spiritual *sādhanā.* It is meditation alone through which the true nature of spiritual existence is perceived. It centralises the scattered powers of life and reveals the internal and infinite powers of consciousness. It is the explosion of the perfection of the spiritual power and wakeful state of existence. It purifies our impure powers. It is through meditation that inauspicious current of consciousness is transformed into auspicious one. In the words of scriptures, all the inauspicious and auspicious currents of consciousness in the end metamorphose into pure state. As the light destroys darkness so meditation destroys perversions. Perversions are active till the consciousness is asleep. As soon as it awakens the spiritual existence attain complete rejuvenation and an extraordinary silent and indivisible current of tranquility starts flowing in the inner soul. When the consciousness awakens there exists neither tension, nor pain, nor sorrow, nor duality. There remain no trace of either mental agitation or intellectual perplexity. Meditation is the infallible cause of the awakening of consciousness; virtually awakening itself is meditation.

Sorrow, despondency, agitation and worry all these exist because very few people possess right vision to look at their own faults. Mostly they charge their companions, sometimes nature, sometimes environment and sometimes even God. Everybody looks towards others, none towards himself. If he neutrally sees himself and auspicious and inauspicious happenings all around, their duality and agitation cannot exist. Meditation means correctly observing one's own self inwardly and neutrally. Being free from attachment and malice if one neutrally looks at all the auspicious and inauspicious happening regarding happiness and sorrow, respect and insult, loss and gain, life and death nothing remains to be done. This is meditation. Neutral observation of pure self is internal absorption.

Mahāveer's *sādhanā* was the sādhanā of meditation. His penance enjoys high reputation in history; there it has been described in detail. But on delving deep, here also importance of meditation is to be seen. His penance was for meditation. This is why wherever the description of his penance comes there is written 'Lord was absorbed in meditation'. First is the posture-steadiness of body, then, silence steadiness of speech and then meditation-steadiness of mind. This was the order of his meditation. In the course of penance meditation was attained and in the course of meditation, inner absorption, penance was performed. If the fact is clearly analysed we see that meditation itself is penance. In the words of the Lord, fasts etc. are external penance. They are related to the body. First inviting bodily hunger and then to bear it, is the process of external penance. Meditation is internal penance, penance of mind and emotions, descent and absorption of self into self. This soul ward *sādhanā* of meditation gradually became normal, self-absorption increased, duality, unsteadiness and despondency were reduced and immutably indifference quietude and non-attachment developed. In the life of Mahāveer there came terrible occasions of agitation, pain and duality but he remained undisturbed. This was possible because he was a true meditator and neutral observer of good or bad happenings. In the bitter contexts of insult and dishonour as well as in mellifluous moments of honour and respect his inner consciousness ever remains unchanged, neutral and non-attached. During all the situations he was simply a looker-on, neither doer nor enjoyer. Outwardly he appeared as a doer and enjoyer but virtually he was not so. The doer or enjoyer lives in the state of duality. It is only the onlooker who gets the light of pure and duality-free knowledge of consciousness.

His philosophy of equality centred on meditation was his own self-inspired innate philosophy. It was neither imposed nor taught by anybody nor read in scriptures. So Mahāveer never said, "May anybody say or do anything, the order of my teacher or scripture is that both in slander and praise, pleasure and pain, loss and gain I should remain unruffled." From the knowledge imposed or borrowed true placidity does not rise. Only in the state of freedom from duality one sees equality and identity everywhere, inside and outside. In the state of non-attachment all the dualistic differences vanish and there remains no trace of dismay distraction, anxiety and perplexity. An unbroken current of bliss and strength starts flowing. All this is nothing but the miracle of meditation.

Mahāveer's meditation was based on the pure knowledge of self. There was no imposed aim, indifferences and unconcern in it. There was nothing like this, "There is much sorrow, great pain, what I should do, how I can be free from them, it would be very good if pleasure is got, liberation is attained so that freedom from pain is achieved; the world is very bad, here none is one's own, all are selfish, cunning and trappens in illusion and delusion." All this is low-level view, designated by the Lord as *ārtadhyāna.* In the *sādhanā* of meditation based on pure knowledge of self and discretion awakens the sense of non-attachment and the light of equality starts sparkling leading to the realisation of soul in respect of the world and liberation. There is neither malice in respect of the world nor infatuation in that of liberation.

True knowledge gives birth to meditation and true meditation to true knowledge. This current flowing from knowledge to meditation and from meditation to knowledge later on merges in the infinite ocean of innate and intuitive bliss.

Meditation is the *sādhanā* to realise pure bliss. Deeper the meditation deeper shall be the bliss attained. Mahāveer walked on this internal path of meditation. Outwardly there were penance, renunciation and many more things but inside there was only meditation, nothing else. Outer fetters can be broken in other ways also, but meditation alone can break the inner fetters. Through meditation Mahāveer got divine bliss and knowledge and attained liberation. From such a purelight, superceding that of the sun, emanates as has been guiding thousands of *sādhakās* in the past, is guiding in the present and shall be guiding in the future.

In respect of attaining the fruit of meditation there is no question of time-interval. It is not so that meditation takes place now and its result comes in far off future. Meditation is an instantaneous *sādhanā.* As soon as there is meditation *nirjarā* comes, fetters break away and the soul is liberated. As soon as there is light, darkness vanishes, it cannot exist even for a moment. True development exists in fullness, not in incompleteness. Meditation is virtually the path of this full development. Mahāveer's meditation aimed at this full development.

A question may arise : "Why Mahāveer took so long a period of twelve and half years in his *sādhanā.* Meditation results in instantaneous realisation then why this delay?". The answer is that at the beginning his meditation had not reached that state of inner absorption, intensity and speed as was required to attain liberation. This is why he remained strict so long in the initial stages of purification and could not achieve desired object. Outer penances were severe and speedy but then there was no pungency in meditation. Stage of inner absorption came and deepened by and by and meditation caught the speed and instaneously his inner world got filled with the divine light of liberation. The work not completed in years, came to be completed in a few moments.

# Concept of Guṇasthāna, Action, Liberation, Soul and Matter in Jainism

11

*P. C. Jain*

In the course of his onward journey on the spiritual path an aspirant has to pass through several phases of evolution before he succeeds in reaching the destination. These phases may be viewed as important landmarks and are indicative of the significant fact that spiritual ascent is a steady and gradual process rather than a sudden jump from the base to the top. The Jain saints and seers analysed in the light of their profound knowledge the phenomenon of inner transformation culminating in supreme realisation and divided the entire span of growth into fourteen stages, called *Guṇasthāna,* based on the qualitative conditions of the soul. The concept of Guṇasthāna is a novel contribution of the Jain School of thought in the realm of philosophy and explains in detail as to how inward changes take place at different levels of spiritual unfoldment. For a clear understanding of this approach it is necessary to be familiar with the basic postulates of Jainism in general and the doctrine of *Karma* in particular. An attempt is made in the following lines to the concepts that go into the making of the whole edifice of Jain metaphysics.

Jainism places all the six substances constituting the universe into two categories, *Jīva* and *Ajīva* or living and non-living.

Whereas the first category includes only the soul, the second one comprises five substances, namely *Pudgala* (matter), *Ākāśa* (space), *Kāla* (time), *Dharma* (motivation or the medium of motion) and *Adharma* (ceasation or the medium of rest). Of these the latter four are inactive and do not play any role in the scheme of spiritual evolution though they are held important for existence of the world-process. Thus soul on the living side and matter on the non-living side are the two substances that have to be studied and enquired into in this context.

Soul embodies consciousness, bliss, knowledge, perception and prowess etc. but matter is devoid of these characteristics. Matter can be known through the senses for it can be perceived, felt, tasted, smelt, heard, weighed and put to chemical test. On the contrary, soul cannot be comprehended by sensory knowledge because it is a formless and transcendent reality unlike the matter which has got a form and is transient. The universe or the creation is the outcome of the interaction of soul and matter. Pure soul feels no impetus and matter ramaining aloof and away from soul is also inert. It is, in fact, the agile association of the above two substances which is responsible for bringing the created world or the *Saṁsāra* into existence. That is why Jainism does not ascribe the creative function to any Supreme being in the form of a personified God but holds that the creative process is inherent in the combination of animate and inanimate substances, viz., spirit and matter. Besides, it cannot be supposed that at some point of time soul existed in its purest form, because if it were ever so, there was no compelling necessity for soul to participate in the worldly game by assuming a material form, i.e., the physical body. The inevitable conclusion which we arrive at is that soul and the matter have been in association with each other since the time immemorial and that they shall continue to be so until soul detaches itself completely from the impact of matter. According to Jain philosophy the world is eternal with no beginning and end and having no external cause of its origin.

Soul possesses immense potentialities of perception, knowledge, bliss and strength etc. but these various faculties get blurred and remain unmanifested due to the covering provided by matter. To what extent soul's latent powers are blocked depends on how intense the material veil is. By means of spiritual discipline soul is enabled to revert to its original pure state after getting itself rid of obscurities of many kinds engendered by matter. It is noteworthy here that matter is incapable of exerting any influence on the soul unless it gets inseparably mixed with it like milk and water. Since soul is formless the influx of matter caused into it must be of most subtle nature for no gross element can assimilate itself into a subtle and formless identity. The fine and invisible particles of matter getting merged with soul are referred to by the word *Karma* in the Jain doctrines. In the common usage *Karma* simply means an action, but it is given a special meaning in the Jain literature dealing with matters spiritual where it stands for that minute mass of matter containing a force of its own which gets attracted to the soul in the wake of an action performed through the media of body, speech and mind. Every action of *Jīva,* physical, oral and mental, is instrumental in drawing certain types of material molecules which, due to the passions of *Jīva,* are immediately absorbed by soul and which once deposited there play restrictive role during the period of their potency. After a certain time, on its fruition or before fruition, an accumulated *Karma* is rendered ineffective but its place might have been taken by a fresh one. Thus there is an ever continuing inflow and outflow of the karmic matter with its due consequence on soul. This is precisely the cause of the worldly existence during which the spirit is suppressed and tormented by the occasional onslaughts of the alien matter.

The *Karmas* are classified into the following eight groups which are so named as to describe their capacity to cause obstruction to all the different faculties of the soul :

1. *Jñānāvaraṇīya* or the knowledge obstructing group;
2. *Darśnanvaraṇīya* or the forces that obstruct with perception;
3. *Vedanīya* or the class of energies which determine the experiencing of pleasure and pain;

4. *Mohanīya* or the forces which produce delusion;
5. *Āyuḥ* or the forces determining the duration of association of soul with a particular physical body;
6. *Nāma* or the energies which organise the body and its limbs;
7. *Gotra* or the energies which determine the family, surroundings, position and the like of individuals; and
8. *Antarāya* or the group of forces which interfere with our doing what we should like to do.

It is evident from the above description that the karmic forces not only weave and design the physical, intellectual and psychological fabric of an individual's personality but also determine such matters as appearance and complexion of the body, voice, longevity, parentage, fortune and the extent of pleasure and pain to be experienced by him. What is commonly known as destiny or fate is actually nothing but the cumulative result of all the varied accumulated *karmas* which were once drawn and absorbed by an individual soul and which got fructified in the due course of time. Man can, therefore be called to be the maker and master of his fate for he can, by his own actions, mould his future extending ever the present as well as the subsequent births.

Though all the *karma*-particles are substantially of the same material stock they acquire differing capabilities according to the particular form which they assume. For example, if certain *karma* particles are reduced to the *Jñānāvaraṇiya* group of *karmas* their action on the spirit will be different from what it will be when they are formed into some other group. No doubt, their function in both the cases will be obstructive, but the nature of obstruction caused shall vary. There is nothing peculiar in this for we are well aware of the fact that bio-chemical process contained in the physical organism reduces the same food into flesh, blood, bones, muscles and marrow etc. Similarly, it is owing to the self-generating mechanism inherent in the *karma*-particles that they get converted into varied forms.

*Jñānāvarṇiya, Darśnanvaraṇiya, Mohanīya* and *Antarāya* are called *Ghātiā* or major *karmaś* for their impact on the spirit is more intense and durable and because they are more difficult to eradicate. The remaining four *karmas* are known as *Aghātiā* or minor *karmas* because they do not greatly overshadow the natural attributes of the soul and can therefore be won over with less difficulty.

Each group of *karmas* consists of a number of energies or forces which may be likened to the various modes or weapons stored in the armoury of a warrior. These energies, technically referred to as *Karma-prakṛtis* in the parlance of Jainism, are found elaborately discussed and described in the Jain texts dealing with this subject. Their numerical strength is shown in the table given below under the *Ghātiā* and *Aghātiā* divisions :

| | *Group of Karmas* | *No. of Energies* | | |
|---|---|---|---|---|
| | | *Ghātiā* or | *Achātiā* | |
| 1. | *Jñānāvarṇiya* | 5 | – | |
| 2. | *Darśnāvarṇīya* | 9 | – | |
| 3. | *Vedanīya* | – | 2 | |
| 4. | *Mohanīya* | 28 | – | |
| 5. | *Āyuḥ* | – | 4 | |
| 6. | *Nāma* | – | 93 | |
| 7. | *Gotra* | – | 2 | |
| 8. | *Antarāya* | 5 | – | |
| | Total : | 47 | 101 | = 148 |

Mention may also be made here of the different phases of the *Karmic* process from the beginning to the end. According to the Jain theory the entire process is comprised of five steps or circuits which are named as *Āśrava, Bundha, Samivara, Nirjarā* and *Mokśa.*

*Āśrava* means the inflow or influx of the karmic matter drawn by an individual soul owing to its physical, oral and mental activity. *Bundha* or bondage represents accumulation and deposition of the drawn-in foreign matter consequent on its absorption by the soul due to passions like anger, pride, deceit and greed. *Samvara* stands for blocking of the channels of influx to bar the entry of fresh *karma* particles resulting in the diminution of the stock of the deposited stuff. *Nirjarā* means a gradual removal of the karmic layers accumulated over the spirit. Some *karmas* are rendered ineffective in the natural course when they fall off due to maturity whereas in case of others efforts are necessary if their shackles have to be cut off before their due time. These two types of *Nirjarā* are known as *Akām-Nirjarā* and *Sakāma Nirjarā* respectively. *Mokśa* is the last step in soul's emancipation when it finally shakes off the last remnants of the *karma* particles and having thus attained the state of absolute purity frees itself for ever from the bondage of birth and death, i.e.., the cyclic a transmigration.

The gamut of *karmas* can be well illustrated by the simile of a reservoir where accumulation of water is constantly taking place due to a greater inflow than out-flow. The inflow is *Āśrava* and the resultant increase in the volume of water is Bandha. If it is desired that the volume of stored up water in the reservoir should gradually diminish, obviously the inlets will have to be narrowed down or blocked and the outlets widened so that less water is pumped in and more is pumped out. This is *Samvara.* It is also evident that some water is being evaporated in the natural course, and if drainage is also arranged simultaneously the task of emptying the reservoir will surely be speeded up. The former is *Akām Nirjarā* and the latter is *Sakāma Nirjarā.* If the above processes involving both the natural evaporation and the drainage continue, soon comes a time when the reservoir gets fully dried up and this is the state of *Mokśa* or liberation or salvation.

In order to arrive at his journey's end the aspirant has to cross all the several stations lying on the way just as a would be graduate is required to cover and complete the prescribed syllabus before he is awarded the degree.

The main features of each of the fourteen stations or *Guṇasthānas* are discussed below:

1. ***Mithyātva***—This is the first stage in evolution marked by gross ignorance in which the soul remains engulfed and for that

reason can not appreciate the pure truth. In this Guṇasthāna certain *prakṛtis* of the Mohaniya *Karma* are temporarily subsided, which state is technically termed as temporary quiescence and which is sure to pass out within a short time. It would be of lasting benefit for the *jīva* if by virtue of his past good actions he comes out of this stage and resolves to make efforts to escape from misery and pain of the worldly life.

2. ***Sasadan***—This stage is characterised by exhausted faith due to which the soul is in the act of falling from the right faith. The duration of this stage is also very short.

3. ***Miśra***—The soul in this stage horers between certainty and doubt about faith. The right conviction evolved out earlier gets diluted with uncertainty. The mental state of the *jīva* being marked by a mixture of *Samayaktva* and *Mithyātva*, right faith and false faith, this *Guṇasthāna* is known as *Miśra* or mixed.

4. ***Avirata Samyagdṛisti***—This stage is arrived at when the aspirant's doubts are removed by meditation or/and by the instructions received from a preceptor. He acquires right faith but because he is not observing necessary vows he is known as *Avirat* (vowless) *Samyagdriṣti.* The karma-*prakritis* momentarily subdued in the first stage are now either partially or wholly subdued or destroyed. This accounts for a definite improvement in the mental state of the jiva.

5. ***Deśavirata***—The aspirant in this stage starts making a beginning in observance of right conduct. As vows are observed here only in part and not in full, this is known as *deś* (part) *vrata* (vows). Some more *karma-prakritis* are subdued or destroyed here.

6. ***Pramatta Virata***—Here the right conduct is slightly tinged with imperfection. This is the first step of life as *muni* or ascetic. The aharak Śarir Prakriti becomes nascent at this stage.

7. ***Apramatta Virat***—The conduct of the *muni* at this stage is perfect without the slightest negligence.

8. ***Apurva Karan***—The conduct of the *sādhak* being perfect he makes further progress in pure meditation (*Śukla* Dhyāna) and is enabled to shake off a few more *karma-prakṛitis.*

9. ***Anivirta Karan***—Here the thought activity of the *muni* is more advanced and refined than in the previous stage.

10. ***Sūkśma Sampraya***—This stage is still superior and is marked by absence of delusion, anger, pride and deceit. All the four types are completely eradicated and only the slightest form of greed remains to be destroyed.

11. ***Upaśānta Moha***—This stage arises due to quiescence or subsidence of the energies of the *Mohanīya Karma,* one of the most powerful *Karmas* to destroy.

12. ***Kśīṇa Moha***—Complete eradication of the *Mohanīya Karma* is the chief characteristic of this stage. It is but natural that with the extinction of this particular major *karma* the soul proceeds towards greater illumination.

It is pertinent to note here that the path bifurcates at the end of the seventh stage, one known as upasama śreṇī or the quiescent route and the other as Kāśāyika Śreṇī or the eradicative route. In the former the *Karma-prakritis* are subdued whereas in the latter these are destroyed. The saint who reaches the eleventh stage keeps travelling backward and forward and consequently falls back to a lower stage. But one who does not feel content with half-way measures and is bent upon full eradication adopts the Kṣāyikaroute which enables him to skip over direct to the twelfth stage without stopping at the eleventh.

13. ***Sayog Kevalī.***—This stage arises on the destruction of all the four major karmas, but association with the body is still retained due to the operation of some of the minor karmas. It is called Sayog because the three channels of activity, viz., body, speech and mind, are not yet extinct. The soul in this stage surpasses all worldly considerations though it survives in the world. This is what is sometimes described as the stage of jiwannukti i.e., salvation while being in the world. Those rare souls who evolve out the Tirthankara prakriti at the thirteenth stage become the Tirthankara or the master who, being fit and ready for the purpose, reveals the true path to the worldly beings for their eternal good. The language in which instructions come

from the Tirthankara is called Anakśri or wordless and admits of no barriers so far appreciation of its inner purport is concerned. For the benefit of human beings it is interpreted in popular diālect by a competent disciple of high calibre (Gandhara). It is worth mentioned that the Mohniya Karma was so long the greatest stumbling block in the manifestation of omniscience (Keval Jñān), and since this Karma has been fully destroyed the faculty of omniscience appears and shines in its fullest bloom without any hindrance or obstruction. One attaining this stage is called Arihant.

14. ***Avoga Kevalī***—This is the last stage on the path which is attained on the demolition of the remaining Aghatia or minor Karmas due to which the yoga or the channels of activity were retained. The soul now ascends to Nirvana, the summit, and transcends the limitations of birth and death. One, who attains this stage, is called Siddha who is absolutely free from the karmic impurity and remains ever established in Right faith, Right knowledge and Right conduct. The ideal of perfection having been fully realised nothing more is now left to be attained.

It needs mention here that the *karma-prakritis* referred to above are three dimensional in character or they may be said to possess three main facts of their working. These are called *Bandha, Satta* and *Udaya* respectively. *Bandha* or bondage contracts a liability on the part of the soul to undergo a certain experience at some future time, either distant or immediate. As said earlier, the actions of various sorts bring the *karma*-particles but these cannot be absorbed by the soul unless it is afflicted with passions like anger, pride, deceit and greed, the intensity and duration of bondage depending upon the degree and extent of the soul's affliction. It is a common knowledge that dust particles brought by the wind produce almost no damaging effect if the surface of the wall happens to be dry, but its effect will certainly be more damaging on a damp surface and will prove to be devastating if the surface is heavily coated with a strong adhesive. So, it is the intensity of passions that actually determines the strength of the bondage. Satta denotes total potentiality of the *karma-prakṛitis* i.e., their overall impact or the maximum extent of their effect on the spirit. By nature all the *karma-prakṛitis* i.e., their overall impact or the maximum extent of their effect on the spirit. By nature all the *karma-prakṛriis* do not ripen at one and the same time and some of them may be kept in abeyance by their counteracting forces and it is only when their influence wanes that the contracted liability turns into reality. Udaya implies fruition and the consequential ineffectiveness of the *karma-prakritis.* Having played their due role by producing a pleasant or unpleasant experience the *karma-prakritis* lose their further operative capacity and become extinct.

Really speaking, the classification of the stages of spiritual evolution into fourteen Guṇasthānas is the study of *karma-prakritis* in terms of their *Bandha, Satta* and *Uday.* The advanced mathematical calculation in this respect as shown by eminent authors is as enchanting as abstruse; and ancient scriptures like the *Gammatasāra* contain a wealth of information on the subject. The scope of the present introductory essay, however, does not permit inclusion of more intricate details. Suffice it to say in retrospect that our actions done in the hoary past as well as in the present, are the sole determinants of our personality in various births, and that by improving the nature and course of those actions we can definitely succeed in placing ourselves in ever better and congenial surroundings and can ultimately free the spirit from the fetters provided by the foreign matter.

## Action

The Jain School of thought is recognised to be an important branch of Indian Philosophy for it has made in this realm many a rich and original contribution, the doctrine of Karma being one of them. The Karmic theory as developed in the Jain methphysics is quite rational and scientific in its approach and analysis and convincingly explains the mechanics of the world, i.e., the motive force behind the cycle of births and deaths. Such a systematic, thorough and comprehensive study of the forces at work in the universe is not found in any other philosophical system, either of the East or of the West. The doctrine of Karma also proves beyond doubt as to why the concept of God as the creator of the world and the ruler of our destiny is wholly untenable and redundant and that the state of godhood can be conceived even without ascribing to it those specific attributes. In fact, this doctrine may be viewed as the foundation on which rests the entire edifice of Jain religion which proposes to enquire what the man's present imperfection is due to and how his state of affairs can be improved upon so that he may succeed in reaching the zenith of perfection.

For a clear understanding of the Karma-doctrine it is necessary for us to comprehend the two basic elements, soul and matter. The substance embodying consciousness, knowledge and bliss etc. is called soul, and the element which is devoid of these characteristics is called matter. The world, as we see it, is nothing but the outcome of interaction of soul and matter because a pure soul feels no impetus, and the matter which is aloof from soul is also incapable of producing any results. The process named world of Samsara begins when soul and matter in unison with each other play an active role by indulging in multifarious physical and mental activities giving rise thereby to varied emotions, impulses and attitudes. It can not be supposed that at some point of time soul existed in its purest form and later on got polluted or contaminated by sin or vice, for if it was over so, soul would have never appeared on the scene as an active agent. The inevitable conclusion that one may arrive at in this respect is that soul and matter have been associated with each other from the time immemorial and that their agile association is responsible for everything worldly. This fact establishes the eternity of creation as well as the falsity of the notion that as a personal being created the world at His will.

That people think it worthwhile to undergo some sort of spiritual discipline in conformity with their faiths and beliefs is indicative of the truth that they do not consider their present state of being as satisfactory and look forward to attaining a higher and nobler one with a view to get rid of their sorrows and sufferings. It can not be denied that the gross sensual pleasures resulting from the material objects offer no solution for sooner or later their reverse trends invariably follow. Moreover, the bodily structure itself, through which all sensual pleasures are enjoyed, is subject to decay and death. This implies that man will have to go beyond the material and the gross for finding out the perennial source of joy. The goal of the man's quest thus having been resolved the next important question arises with regard to the means and procedure by the adoption of which the desired goal can be achieved. Jainism answers to this by forwarding a simple logic that since the world with all its paraphernalia has been brought about by the union of soul and matter, it can be negated through the process of dis-union of these two components. That means separation of matter from soul is the pre-requisite for the full manifestation of soul's potentialities in the same way as shifting of chaff becomes necessary for ensuring the quality of food-grains. It would be pertinent to note here that the Jain tradition holds that process alone as the truly religious process which helps man regain the original and indestructible faculties of soul by ridding it of the impact of matter which causes several kinds of obscurities and keeps it (soul) in bondage.

Kanna may be defined as the fine and invisible particles of matter, having force or energy, that are constantly drawn to soul during the course of its journey from one incarnation to another. Every action, whether good or bad, and whether physical or mental, opens the door to certain kinds of particles of matter which may immediately enter into union with soul. Even when from matter does not come from out-side, there is always a sufficient amount of it present in the physical organism itself that can be readily absorbed by the soul. The stock of both the existing and influenced matter is technically known as the Sarmaṇ Sharira which does not perish on the death of the physical body but accompanies soul in the subsequent births. The Sarmaṇ Sharira thus acts as a self-adjusting prison for soul, and the Karmic force contained therein conditions the physical body and other circumstances such as family, status and wealth etc. that soul will have in its worldly existence from birth to birth. This justifies the theory that soul transmigrates and that life does not come to naught simply on the demolition of the physical frame in which soul was encased for same time.

As the same food gets formed into flesh, blood, muscles, bones and marrow etc., so are the different kinds of karmic energies engendered from the particles of matter absorbed by soul. Of the eight Karmas, the first, second, fourth and eighth are called Chetia (destroyers) or the major karmas because they obstruct the natural qualities of the spirit and the remaining four as Aghatia or minor because of their not interfering with those attributes.

The whole gamut of the Karmic process from the beginning to the end may be said to comprise of the following five stages:

| | |
|---|---|
| (i) Asarva | In-flow of the karmic matter for absorption by soul; |
| (ii) Bundha | Fusion of the flowed in matter with the spirit; |
| (iii) Samvara | Stoppage of fresh influx of matter; |
| (iv) Nirjara | Gradual removal of matter and consequent destruction of karmic energies by way of natural corporation and individual exertion, and |
| (v) Moksha | Complete freedom of soul from the bondage of matter due to subversion of the karmic force. |

The five stages enumerated above can be well illustrated by the simile of a pond where constant inflow (Asarva) and accumulation (Bandha) of water are taking place. One may also observe that some amount of water in the pond gets evaporated in the natural course and some is drained out through the human efforts (Nirjara). When the inflow ceases (samvara) but the natural evaporation and drainage continue the volume of water remaining in the pond obviously diminishes and if this process continues, soon comes a time when the pond gets fully dried up.

The foregone discussion presents but a bare outline of the doctrine of Karma as propounded by the Jain seers and for an elaborate expiration of it the reader is advised to refer to the authoritative texts on the subject. The knowledge of how the karmic forces emerge due to the actions of the jiva, how the particles of matter get dissolved into soul and distort its real image, how the inflow of the foreign matter can be checked and how the layers of karmas accumulated on soul can gradually be removed and finally shaken off, is as much fascinating as stimulating for an aspirant who desires to make a real head-way towards his spiritual upliftment. A due appreciation of this doctrine will certainly induce ill to desist from those actions which attract a heavy mass of karmic matter and weave a thick covering over soul suppressing and hindering thereby its inherent qualities.

Let it be said in recapitulation that our destinations are governed not by an outside agency but by our own karmas or actions and that freedom of soul lies in the total rejection of the foreign matter. Emancipation or salvation (Moksha) in the end of man's spiritual endeavours and this can be attained on complete severance of connection with the Karmic matter which has so far been a part and parcel of soul. Once this stage is reached, soul has no reason to revert to the world to participate in the play of interaction.

## Liberation

The philosophical systems of the orient, by and large, recognise liberation as the be-all and end-all of man's spiritual endeavours, though there is no unanimity of opinion on its precise definition. The Jain School of Thought has dived deep into the matter and has offered a clear and profound exposition of its findings based on inner realisation. According to it, liberation is the highest elevation attained by soul on complete destruction of the eight Karmas which so far held it in subjugation and subjected it to cyclical transmigration. This stage emerges when all doors to bondage are completely shut for ever and when the existing stock of the Karmic stuff is fully exhausted. Thus there are two pre-conditions to liberation, non-existence of the causes of bondage; and the total annulment or shedding of the previously accumulated Karmic matter. On fulfilment of two conditions, which are technically termed as Bandha-hetvabhava and Nirjara respectively, soul is enabled to gain its absolute purity and to shine in the brightest glory of intelligence.

As bondage (Bandha) and shedding (Nirjara) are important postulates in the Jain doctrine of liberation, those need be analysed and understood in their right perspective.

Bandha signifies absorption of the fine and invisible material particles that are drawn to soul in the wake of an action, whether physical, oral or mental. every activity of the jiva causes certain molecules of matter to move towards soul which readily assimilates them if it (soul) happens to be afflicted with passions like anger, pride, deceit and greed. It is noteworthy that mere influx of matter does not bring about bondage unless soul is found in the grip of passions. In other words, it is the passionate activity of mind, speech and body which is actually responsible for causing bondage. Passions act like the adhesive coated on the surface of a wall drawing and absorbing particles of dust. Just as a dry surface remains free from the damaging effects of the dust particles, so also a passion-free soul remains unaffected by the drawn-in foreign matter.

In the vocabulary of the Jain metaphysics the word 'Yoga' refers both to the combination of mind, speech and body and their activity whereas the word 'Kashya' stands for the four passions. The three channels of activity and the passions may be said to be the primary or basic causes of bondage for there shall be no bondage if there is no activity and if soul is not afflicted with passions. The other contributory causes of bondage brought out are three viz. wrong belief (Mithyatva), vowlessness (Avirati) and carelessness (Pramada). This classification of the five causes of bondage brings out as to how the process of degeneration sets in. Evidently one having a wrong notion of reality and suffering from the myopia of vision, can never be serious about the observance of the prescribed vows, which are nothing but the golden rules of conduct. Such a person invariably becomes careless in the conduct of his multifarious affairs. Lack of right perception, coupled with non-observance of the code of conduct and carelessness makes him easily amenable to passions which trait makes him lose all control over his body, speech and mind. In fact, the five causes of bondage as enumerated above are the glaring weaknesses which lead to man's downfall both in the mundane and spiritual spheres.

It is obvious in the light of the above discussion that in order to stop bondage its causes ought to be wholly dispensed with. The aspirant shall perhaps do well by beginning with observance of the necessary vows which will bereave him of his serious drawback of carelessness and laziness. The purity of conduct, born of control over body, speech and mind, will endow him with the right vision which will be instrumental in weakening the force of his passions and in enabling him ultimately to win over them. Passionless activity is assuredly the first step towards non-activity which is but another name for the cessation of 'Yoga'. It needs mention that the upward phase or the process denoting progress has a 'multiplier effect' each component giving support and strength to every other components and thus giving momentum to the entire process, whereas the down-ward phase or the process of degeneration works in a vicious circle where each factor weakens its associates and contributes to the commenting of successive layers of Karmas over soul.

The Gunasthan analysis propounded by the Jain Āchāryas gives a detailed account of the spiritual improvement taking place at different stages of evolution. The whole distance between the points of start and destination has been divided into fourteen stages, named Gunasthanas, the first representing one where the various causes of bondage are fully at work and the last where these become wholly extinct. The 'Yoga' or the channels of activity continues upto the thirteenth stage whereas the kashayas or passions are eradicated by the twelfth. Though the eradication of most intense type of passions starts from the second stage it is only at the twelfth that the last remnants of greed are eradicated. This shows that greed is by far the strongest passion and hence most difficult to eradicate. Mithyatva, Avirati and Pramada are extinct by the seventh stage. There is no doubt that sustained efforts are required on the part of the sādhaka for bringing the process of bondage to a full stop.

Nirjara or shedding denotes removal of shackles of the Karmas that get associated with soul in course of time. The process of purification reaches its zenith at the fourteenth stage and culminates into liberation at which soul transcends all impediments and barriers coming in its way.

**Soul**

Soul is an important concept very elaborately and comprehensively dealt with in the Jain texts and may be said to be the central theme of Jain Religion and Philosophy. It is, in fact, the pivot around which the entire metaphysical system clusters for by virtue of being the only living substance, out of the six that constitute the universe, soul plays a major and decisive role in all spheres and frightfully deserves to be studied in its various aspects. Matter is another non-living substance which, in close and active partnership with soul, contributes to the latter's corporeal existence and transmigratory character. Here, two different forms of soul can be conceived; the impure form which having been associated with the alien matter since the time immemorial transmigrates from one incarnation to another and the pure form which have completely freed itself from the material impact and has transcended the cycle of birth and death. These two forms of soul are also referred to as the Empirical Self and the Ego-in-itself; the wordly soul and the liberated soul; and the Jivātmā and Parmātmā.

In his classical work entitled Samaya-Pahud or Samaya Sara, Āchārya Kunkunda, an eminent and versatile author-philosopher of the first century A.D. has outlined the nature of the pure self as distinguished from the empirical self and has named them as Sva-Samaya and Par-Samaya respectively. According to him, every soul, whether empirical or liberated, is endowed with three main attributes, Darśan, i.e., belief; Jñān, i.e., knowledge; and Charita, i.e., conduct. The worldly soul can not therefore be treated to be intrinsically different from the Ego-in-itself, the former being the contaminated and imperfect version and the latter as refined and perfect version of the same identity. Faculties of Darśan, Jñān and Charita as manifested in a worldly soul are inferior in quality and limited in extent but in a realised or liberated soul these have attained the maximum level of their unfoldment. The empirical self has definitely to pass through a process of refinement so that it can be transformed into the transcendental self by discarding all the upadhic conditions attached to it.

Before discussing the pure and impure forms any further, it would be relevant to know about the general characteristics of soul. Here again, reference may be made to Āchārya Kunkunda's two other principal treatises, viz. Pravacansara and Pencastikaya where the author has discussed this subject. He says in Pravacansara :

**अरसमरुवमगंधं अध्वत्तं चेदणागुणमसद्दं।**
**जाण अलिगंग्गहणं जीवमणिद्दिट्ठसंठाणं॥ ४९॥**

"Soul is an imperceptible substance for it has no taste, no form, and no smell, nor can it be equated to sound, i.e., Sabda (as is believed in by some). It is not the object of inferential knowledge, has no definite shape of its own and possesses consciousness or intelligence as its essential attribute."

The definition given in Pencastikaya is as follows :

**जीवोत्ति हवदिचेदा उवओगविसेसिदो पहू कत्ता।**
**भोत्ता य देहमत्तो ण हि मुत्तो कम्मसंजुत्तो॥ २७॥**

"The soul or jiva is an intelligent being having inherent of qualities of knowledge and perception, it is its own master in the matter of performing various actions and reaps the fruits thereof, its size is proportionate to the body it assumes; and is incorporeal inspite of its being associated with the Karmic matter."

Basing upon the above descriptions, which fully contain the Jain view, the following main points may be noticed regarding the nature, functions and structure of soul :

1. Every living being necessarily has life which is nothing but consciousness expressed through faculties of knowledge and perception. An animate being is named jiva because it knows, perceives and feels. Will, movement and growth are found only in the jiva who fundamentally differs from Pudgala (matter). Matter has sensible qualities such as form, taste, smell and colour but soul or the spirit has none and can not therefore be known by the senses nor by means of inference which draws its sustenance from the sense perception. Logic tells us that the attribute or the quality is inseparable from the object possessing it because one can not exist without the other. For example, fire and ignition speak of the same reality for neither can there be fire without ignition nor ignition without fire. Likewise soul is the same thing as consciousness or its attributes of knowledge and perception. This may be put in the form of an equation thus :

   Jiva—consciousness—knowledge (Gyan) and
   perception (Darśan)

2. Every jiva is responsible for his rise and fall. By his own actions he can enchain himself and can also secure release from bondage. None else than he himself is the cause of his slavery and freedom. He is equally capable of the lowest degradation and the highest ascent and it is in this sense that he is called Prabhu or the master.

3. The soul is designated as Karta for being the generator of thoughts arising out of the various states of karmas it is bound with. Thoughts may emerge due to subsidence of Karmas, due to destruction of Karmas, due to partial subsidence and partial destruction of Karmas, due to fruition of karmas, and in the natural way quite independent of Karmas. It is to be

noted here that Karmas are only the instrumental or indirect cause of thoughts, their main and direct cause being the jiva himself.

4. The soul is also Bhokta, the experiences of pleasure and pain. A feeling is an important fact of consciousness; the jiva must taste the sour and sweet fruits borne of Karmas associated with it.
5. The soul has no definite size of its own but its size is proportionate to the size of the body in which it is encased. The capacity of expansion and contraction contained in soul enables it to adjust to its physical structure. That an elephant's body is very large as compared to that of an ant does not mean that the two souls residing in the two bodies are unequal in size. Despite differences in the outer coverings there is absolutely no difference so far as the inner content is concerned. The soul may be likened to a semifluid jelly which can equally be spread in a smaller or bigger tray. Just as the light expands itself within the area of a place where its source is located, so also soul circumscribes a tiny or large physical body given to it for occupation during a certain incarnation.
6. Though soul is incorporeal by nature it is said to corporeal (Murtik) because of its being associated with matter. The association between soul and matter is not at all superficial but it is by way of complete assimilation and transmutation of the two substances into one compònent. The empirical soul has been in its diluted and distorted form since the beginningless past and shall continue to be so until eternity i.e., so long as the accumulated layers of matter are not wholly scratched away. The invisible material particles are drawn to soul through the three channels of activity, mind, speech and body, due to the four passions like anger, pride deceit and greed. Of the total influx, some of the particles get converted into Karmic forces such as Jñānverniya, Darshanaverniya etc. causing obstruction to the various faculties of soul, whereas some of them undergo merely an organic change with no consequential imbalance created on the personality of the jiva.

Āchārya Kunkunda has considered the position of soul both from practical and real stand points. These view-points need therefore be understood in thei: right perspective to assess the importance underlying them.

The real point of view or the Nischaya Nyāya examines a substance in its original and pure form without emphasising on its modifications which are ever changing. From birth until his death a man undergoes a constant change not only in his organic body but also in his mental make up. Broad changes marked by stages like childhood, adolescence, youth and old age etc. are apparently visible, but the minute changes taking place in a man from moment to moment can not be caught by the naked eye. The entire process of change, which is both continuous and gradual, can neither be perceived nor described. But despite these changes there is something which does not change and remains steady. It is due to this steadiness that the changing object is recognizable. A finger ring may be converted into an ear-ring but the same gold remains present in both the shapes. A child in course of time attains maturity but his identity as one and the same person is not lost. That is why he continues to be called by the same name. It can rightly be said that changes occur only in the conditions or modifications and never in the substance itself. The real point of view or the Nischaya Nyāya examines the substance whereas the examination of the conditions falls within the purview of the practical point of view or the Vyāvahār Naya.

Besides, everything possesses a basic or spontaneous nature which holds true at all times except when it gets distorted due to the influence caused by extraneous elements. Obviously the perverted state continues to exist as long as the foreign influence persists, and on its nullification the original pure state emerges a new. For example, water which by its nature is cool and fluid, becomes hot by coming into contact with heat and turns into ice when it undergoes the process of refrigeration. Undoubtedly, the hot and frozen states of water are only temporary phases because when removed away from heat the hot water cools down after sometime, and the ice also melts when it is kept in the open air.

Similarly, the inherent qualities of soul like perception, knowledge, bliss and strength etc. remain obscured, interrupted and blurred so long as the karmic influence lasts and dominates, but when the alien domination weakens the original pure nature of the self begins to bloom and on its total extinction soul shines in its brightest glory. Āchārya Kunkunda calls the inherent nature as Sva-bhava, for its being self generating and not dependent upon and created by any external force whatsoever and the perverted and alloyed nature as par-bhava for it is the outcome of an outside influence which forces the basic nature to recede to the background. The Niscaya Naya takes cognigence only of sva-bhava leaving aside the par-bhava which actually forms the subject matter of the vyavahar-naya.

In the above background can now be discerned the nature of the empirical ego in its sullen, soiled and fettered state in glaring contrast to the Ego-in-itself which has gained the condition par-excellence and which is a living embodiment of all the natural qualities. In fact, the relationship between the two kinds of self is one of identity-cum-difference, i.e., both are identical and at the same time different. Metaphysically speaking, the empirical self is said to be at par with the super empirical self for its being potent enough to reach the supreme elevation, but considering their current level of development and manifestation they widely differ from each other.

Moreover, comprehension of the lower self presents no difficulty for all are familiar with and are instinctively engaged in the mundane pursuits of life. On the other hand, realisation of the higher self is not so easy as it implies turning the highest ideal into reality and requires sustained and sincere efforts to be made in the right direction. While the upadhic conditions brought about by Karmas have been attached to the empirical self since an indeterminable past, these are wholly non-existent in the transcendental self. Therefore the characteristics of soul that are spoken of from the practical point of view will not be exactly similar to those that hold good from the real point of view. In other words, of the general characteristics of soul discussed earlier, some are attributable to the empirical self and some to the super empirical self. According to Jain Philosophy as and when soul gets rid of the last remnants of the Karmic matter, which has hitherto been a part and parcel of it, the channels of activity, i.e.., body, speech and mind, are reduced to nothingness and all the physical and psychical functions automatically come to naught. Consequently the liberated soul no longer admits of its role as Prabhu or the master in performing good or bad actions; as Karta or the generator of various types of thoughts; as Bhokta or the experiencer of pleasure and pain; and gives up once for all its identity as Murtik or a corporeal being. Now, soul, in its transcendental state, is nothing but pure consciousness ever established in the right faith, right knowledge and right conduct. It is the empirical self which is characterised as the door of actions, as the enjoyer of the fruits of actions, and as a corporeal being for constantly drawing and absorbing the Karmic and non-karmic matter.

Āchārya Kunkunda proclaims that Sva-Samaya or the absolutely pure soul is the summum bonum, the pinnacle of perfection, the loftiest summit, and the most sublime ideal to be aimed at and strived for by the jivatma who is tossed to and fro in the whirlwinds of the Sansaric career and is made to bear all the consequential pains and miseries. He asserts that it is erroneous to identify the true self either with the empirical self or with the outer cosmos consisting of matter, the principles of motion and rest, time, space and other souls. To put it otherwise, every soul is different not only from the non-living objects but also from other living organism present in the human society and the rest biological kingdom. It is for this reason that Jain metaphysics does not subscribe to the idea of mass consciousness or world consciousness which offers only a subsidiary existence to the individual souls. It is maintained that the physical and the psychical states belong only to the empirical ego, the super-empirical ego being totally devoid of them. For further clarification the Acharya states that soul mixed with Karmic and non-karmic matter, and attuned with the upadhic conditions cannot be taken for the real self in the same way as all mineral ore can not be accepted for pure gold. Since each substance has its own independent existence, the original character of one can only be influenced and can never be determined by any other substance which gets associated with it. Accordingly, all that has been imprinted and embossed by the foreign matter can not be passed for the genuine nature of soul. The great Āchārya also emphasizes that unlike the empirical self the Ego-in-itself can not be graded or classified for it is a class by itself and is entirely free from the Karmic effects materialising in the form of mental states such as desire, aversion and delusion etc. as well as in the form of organic body with different colours, shapes and skeleton structures.

## Matter

Matter may be said to be the base of creation. All that is touchable, tasteble, smellable, perceivable and audible is essentially material in character. Having properties of form, taste, smell and colour matter is perceptible to senses and can be felt by contact and palate, smelt, perceived and heard. Sound is also material for it is produced by concussion of material objects, can be captured in a tape and released later on. Matter can well be comprehended by inference. For example, on seeing smoke one can easily infer that there is fire somewhere, because emission of smoke must definitely be due to fire. However, the inferential knowledge can be applied to matter alone. In other words, by means of inference only matter can be known, a non-material entity being totally beyond the scope of inference. Unlike the spirit, matter is devoid of consciousness and has no will, movement and growth of its own.

Matter can initially be grouped into two categories, the one which retains its independent existence, and the other which merges with soul. The former is a combination of molecules appearing in innumerable shapes such as textiles, paper, plastic products, metallic goods, wares, furniture and houses etc., but the latter gives up its separate identity when mixed up with soul. The second category is again bifurcated into what are technically known as no-Karmas and Karmas respectively. The material particles which undergo bio-chemical change and get reduced to bodily structure are termed as no-karmas. On the other hand, Karmas are those fine material particles which assume invisible form on being absorbed by soul, like a sponge soaking the colour mixed in water, and overshadow its inherent faculties. Just as black clouds block the vision, the material particles forming themselves into Karmic forces act as a veil over the natural qualities of the spirit. It is thus evident that the word 'Karma' has a special connotation in the parlance of Jainism where it stands for the degrading force contained in the foreign bodies that have entered into soul. It is to be noted that though both no-Karmas and Karmas are drawn from the same material stock, they differ from each other in respect of their capacity to cause obstruction. As stated earlier, no-Karmas simply go into the making of physical organism and have no further role to play, but Karmas put stumbling blocks in the spirit's way and hinder manifestation of its inherent attributes of knowledge, perception, bliss and strength etc.

Jainism as a spiritual discipline has studied with greater stress the Karmic aspect of matter and has analysed its manifold impact felt by soul. Notwithstanding the fact that the ancient Jain authors have elaborately dealt with the physical aspect of matter, they have mainly concentrated on its Karmic aspect high-lighting the point that for enjoying eternal bliss soul must rub out all marks imprinted and embossed by the matter with which it has been in association since as indeterminable past. That the Jain religion aims at separating the alien matter having characteristics diametrically opposite to those of the spirit is amply proved by the code of conduct prescribed for ascetics and the house-holders. The soul, which is an imperceptible substance without any form, taste, smell and colour, has lost its intrinsic purity owing to the contamination produced by the diluted matter and it is for this reason that it takes up a physical frame in every incarnation and changes it for a new one on its decay. Thus each mundane soul is subjected to birth and death. This process of transmigration continues until soul is completely free from the material pollution and attains an absolutely pure state-which is the state of liberation.

The Jain theory of creation rests on this important premise that the created world with all its paraphernalia is nothing but a projection of matter combining either with itself or with the spirit. The world, as we see it, consists of inanimate objects and animate beings. The inanimate objects include things from a tiny alpine to huge structures like the sky scrappers. Being lifeless these are undoubtedly material. The animate part of the world comprises the whole biological kingdom pulsating with life such as vegetation, insects, birds, animals, aquatics and mankind etc. It is common knowledge that all beings in the animate world have not attained the same stage in evolution. Whereas some of them like human beings are highly developed, both physically and mentally, others are found at the lower levels of the ladder. For example, animals like monkeys, elephants and lions, though quite developed physically, are unable to speak a language. Still there are so many others who have not reached even that level of physical development, what to say of the sophisticated organs like the psyche and the mind. So, the variations that are actually found in the animate world are nothing but the variations in the physical, psychological and mental development of the beings. At this point a pertinent question arises as to what these differences are due to. As pure souls do not admit of any difference whatsoever, the differences that exist in the worldly souls must necessarily be due to the different material composition in them. In case these souls were free from the impact of matter, no disparities of any kind could arise between two individuals. The other philosophical systems provide no satisfactory answer to this complex question. They either evade it on the ground of fate or destiny, or co-relate it with some extraneous factors. The Jain School of thought alone solves the riddle in an unambiguous manner by saying that it depends upon the quantum, magnitude variety and shape of the invisible material particles absorbed by a particular soul as to how it will fare in its mundane career. In fact, the Karmic forces weave and design the entire fabric of a jiva's personality and determine all matters such as the extent of one's knowledge, perception and prowess, parentage, body's structure and complexion, voice and longevity etc. The doctrine of Karma as propounded by the adepts in the spiritual science clearly demonstrates how significantly matter reacts while remaining a part and parcel of soul. Jainism does not, therefore, subscribe to the view that God is the creator of the universe and maintains that Godhood can be attained only when the soul's partnership with matter is dissolved for good and when its participation in the game of interaction, e.g., the creative process, altogether ceases.

The prominence of matter in creation can be explained yet from another perspective. The world may be conceived in its external and internal aspects. The external world is what we see around us, the world where we live, move and act. This world is full of the non-living objects and the living beings. All the lifeless object are wholly material because their bodily structure is made of matter but the living beings also draw heavily upon the material objects for support and sustenance. Be it food for satisfying hunger, or cloth for protection and decoration of the body or house for living or medicine for curing ailments, a living being can not do without the aid and assistance of things material. Thus matter contributes in a major way to the constitution and composition of the external world.

The internal world does not exist in reality but is the creation of thoughts and imagination. Despite this the internal world is in no-way less perfect in its details and may even be more picturesque than the real world. The world appearing in dreams provides a good example of how strange the imaginary world can be as compared to the world in reality. In the course of evolution the developed beings have acquired two finer faculties, namely the psyche and the mind.

The psyche enables one to feel and the mind to think. Emotions and thoughts in their dimensions and variations emanate from these sophisticated instruments which have evolved out of matter. All the psychic and mental conditions are therefore material because their source itself, e.g., the psyche and the mind, happens to be material. If association with matter is desired to be shunned, one shall be required to control one's thoughts and emotions.

Meditation is considered to be a potent source of spiritual enlightenment for it helps check the flow of thoughts and enables the aspirant to disassociate himself with matter, atleast to some extent. How far the meditation practised by one has been effective and meaningful can be judged by the extent one has been successful in soaring high in the realm of thoughtlessness.

So, from whatever angle the proposition is examined, we reach the conclusion that matter plays a very significant role in the process .of creation. The material particles absorbed by individual souls not only shape and design the outer physical organs but also determine the extent of their internal capacity. Just as varying degrees of voltage of electric current may be released at different points, varied kinds of influences may be exerted by matter, depending upon the nature and variety of the particles drawn and absorbed by each soul. The analysis presented by Jain seers proves beyond doubt that emancipation is possible when untoward impressions hitherto created by matter on soul are wholly erased and when the possibility of their further creation is nipped in the bud. The soul that aspires for transcending the vicious circle of birth and death must consciously strive hard to lessen the burden imposed by the diluted matter. For success in this endeavour it is necessary that one should first avoid intense types of physical, verbal and mental actions which bring about a heavy influx of matter and then should gradually try to dispense with the milder ones so that the process of disassociation can ultimately be completed.

that is the nobility of character and deeds that bestows a superior status on a man and not simply his birth in a so-called high caste. Likewise, he did not accept the proposition that a language deserves to be looked down upon only because it is not spoken by the elite. He preferred for his discourses the language spoken by the masses and proved emphatically that the folk-language too had the capacity to express high ideas. Let it be borne in mind that as Mahāveer's opposition was not directed against any particular person or language as such, but against the illogical complex which was responsible for generating feelings of hatred and ill-will and was thereby creating a gulf between man and man. These are but a few instances to show that Mahāveer appeared during his times as a great visionary, a messiah and a prophet who gave to the human race not only lofty ideals to live by but also the new values of life replacing those that had became obsolete and irrelevant.

Of the several facets of Mahāveer's personality, that of a *Mahāyogī* or a great adept in the art and science of *Yoga* shines most prominently. The record of his life's events as found in the authoritative texts composed by saintly authors bears testimony to this. It has to be admitted that Mahāveer's way of *sādhanā* was nothing else than pure *yoga* which duly reflected in all his movements, may in every pore of his being. Not only his body was trained to the utmost to withstand the *vicissitudes* of disease and decay, but he had an absolute control over his senses and mind as well. It is no wonder that he came to be recognised as a living embodiment of all the supreme faculties, including divine attributes (*Riddhis*) and miraculous powers (*Siddhis*) that develop in a man as the result of his fullest spiritual unfoldment and yogic perfection. With complete demolition of four major *Ghātiyā Karmas* Mahāveer's soul had attained the highest state of perfection with the only difference that association with the body was still retained to a nominal degree, and that too for the good of the world at large. This stage in evolution is obviously far superior to that of a worldly human-being and at this the knowledge acquired surpasses all limits of reason and thought because it is perfect and direct (*Pratyakṣa)* and not derived and indirect (*Parokṣa*). In fact this sort of radical transformation marks the zenith of spiritual growth and may be said to be the real culmination of one's spiritual strivings, whether pursued through religion or any other type of discipline.

A close study of the lives of high ranking mystics, seers and founders of religions reveals that there are some traits of character which are found in all of them. These may be enumerated as ecstacy, moral elevation, psychic powers and genius. When the human soul rises to the levels unreached and unexperienced before it transcends the boundaries of mind and gets endowed with many rare gifts by dint of which the master thereof is proclaimed to be a superman, a saviour, a servant. Such a person having felt a stupendous explosion in his being remains absorbed in deep meditation and becomes totally oblivious to the world outside experiencing at the same time the supreme bliss. This transcendent state of ecstacy called *samādhi* does not come in isolation but is invariably associated with elevation of moral standard, emergence of psychic powers like healing by sight and touch etc., and a tremendous increase in literary talents and ability of expression. As a result of the full bloom of his latent faculties the person concerned acquires such capacities that has utterances are fulfilled and that he can read the past and predict the future with precision.

In the Jain tradition, one who has attained omniscience (*Kevalajñāna)* but has not yet attained salvation (*Mokśa*) has been designated a '*Arhat*' and is said to possess many outstanding attributes like complete observance of the principle of non-violence, immunisation against attacks of all kinds, non-requirement of oral food, lack of hunger and thirst, no growth of hairs and nails, no blinking of eyes, walking above ground and ability to communicate thoughts to all beings without hindrances of language. These attributes in their essence are nothing more than elaborated versions of those described earlier viz., ecstacy, elevated moral standards, psychic powers and genius and should not be regarded as imaginary superlatives added by the devotees to their deity. Mention may be made here of the phenomenon of '*divya-*

*dhvani'* ascribed to a *Tīrthaṅkara.* It is believed that all beings attending his discourse can comprehend the truth contained therein irrespective of differences in their mental structures and vocal organs. Let this not be mistaken to be a miracle or supernatural feat but be accepted as a positive proof of the marvellous ability of communication possessed by a genius of Mahāveer's calibre.

A question is sometimes posed about the specific technique or method adopted by Mahāveer for his spiritual realisation. Though no cut and dried formula can be forwarded in answer to this question it may be said without fear of contradiction that Bhagwan laid supreme emphasis on meditation and austere mode of living for attaining purity of the soul and for making steady progress towards inner transformation. This is contrary to the traditional *Hathayoga* where the approach to the spiritual is through the physical. In Mahāveer's way of '*Sādhanā* the entire importance is attached to the training of self signifying sublimation of mind through control of various reflexes as opposed to the training of the body and its limbs. That is why, instead of prescribing any particular postures he prescribed the trinity of right faith, right knowledge and right conduct as the means to attain salvation. Needless to say that the adjective 'right' used with each of the three requisites above is extremely significant. However, *Yoga,* according to him, did not aim at attaining something from outside, may it be called as grace or known by any other name, but it is a device by which the hidden potentialities of the soul are fully developed and manifested. In his opinion, inner transformation leading to spiritual enlightenment is a process by self within self, solely dependent on one's own sincere efforts and not on the aid or assistance provided by an external agency. Not to speak of relying on any one else, he did not look even to the so called God to help him attain the desired spiritual perfection, because he did not conceive god as an outside force or entity supervising from above the worldly affairs below, but by the concept of godhood he meant the essential condition of the soul after it has got itself completely rid of all the various obscurities caused by *Karmas,* which so far blurred its vision and kept its original sterling properties under suppression.

It is perhaps the way of the world that the men of real genius do not get proper appreciation in their life time and are often misunderstood. Mahāveer, too was no exception to this general tendency as he had come to face staunch opposition from many circles. Some abhorred him because his person was not covered, some were antagonistic towards him because their selfish ends were jeopardised by his outspoken statements, some attached to him the stigma of being an atheist without understanding the rationale behind his non-belief in a personified God, while some others shunned him because he propounded and preached a philosophy that was more appealing and convincing than their own. The cumulative result of all this was that despite a good following and commanding a highly honourable position he had to experience tremendous odds in life including assaults on his revered person. Legend has it that once an enraged person tried to push sharp ironnails through his earholes. Considering those times this does not at all appear to be an exaggeration. There might have been many more such catastrophes but the most important point to remember here is that he had in him a perennial source of strength that sustained him to mitigate successfully the evil designs of his opponents. We cannot escape the conclusion that the source of strength under reference was cultivated and nurtured through *Yoga* and by the proper application of this he every time came out unhurt in body and unruffled in mind.

Mahāveer can thus be rightfully proclaimed as a *Mahāyogi* for all the various attributes of a *yogi par excellence* together with numerous yogic achievements found their full expression in his great personality and because by taking recourse to *yoga* he could rise from manhood to Godhood.

The ideas preached by Bhagwan Mahāveer were much in revolt against the established religious conventions and beliefs of that time. Animal sacrifice to please the gods was much in vogue where thousands and thousands of animals were butchered in the good name of religion. Mahāveer, who was horrified to see the atrocities committed on the helpless victims, decided to put a stop to the in-human tortures inflicted upon the innocents as a ritual duly sanctified by religion. He declared that every being in the world enjoys a basic right to live and that no one has the authority to take away that solemn right. His message of love and non-violence found expression in the sacred doctrine of "Live and let live" which says that it is for the sake of our own living that we should allow others to live. These ideas of Bhagwan Mahāveer were not taken up immediately and there was opposition from the vested interests. It was contended for example, that animal sacrifice was sanctioned by the Vedas. Mahāveer's answer to this was that he did not believe in such scriptures which sanctify killing. If it was argued that the Vedas descended right from God and were not to be questioned, Mahāveer's simple answer was that he did not believe in a personified God who either wrote himself or dictated His words contained in the vedic texts. Now, considering those times we can very well appreciate how bold these assertions were which not only doubted the authority of the much "taken for granted" vedic scriptures but also brought about a basic change in the concept of God and Godhood. Another outstanding declaration of Bhagwan Mahāveer was that the status of a man in society should be determined on the basis of his deeds and not of his birth. It is not at all democratic, he said, to confer nobility on one simply because one is born in a noble family. In a society dominated by casteism this was a big revolt and Mahāveer faced opposition on this score also. A third dimension of his astounding reforms was the use of the language of the masses which was looked down upon and was considered to be an improper and inefficient vehicle of thought. Only the language of the elite was thought to be fit and proper to express high ideas. Bhagwan Mahāveer preferred for his discourses the language of the people to bring home to them the ideas he wanted to convey to them. These are only a few instances to show that Bhagwan Mahāveer appeared during his times as a messiah and as a missionary who brought about much needed reforms in society and also gave to the human race new values of life by deleting those which became irrelevent and obsolete.

Every school of thought has two branches, ethics and metaphysics. Whereas ethics relates to the code of conduct, metaphysics refers to the mode of thinking. Looking from that perspective, it may be said that non-violence is the ethical aspect of Jainism and the philosophy of standpoints as its metaphysical aspect. Whatever is found discussed in the vast Jain Literature written by eminent authors is nothing but an elaborate exposition of these two basic concepts of non-violence and the philosophy of standpoints which in fact are one because they stand for the same point of view which is called non-violence in the realm of actions and the philosophy-of-standpoints in the realm of thoughts. As thoughts and actions can not be separated they are to be taken as the two sides of the same coin and therefore are complimentary to each other.

Every object in the world is governed by different relationships which coexist without conflict and contradictions because they are spoken of with reference to different things and not one. A man, for example, may be father, son, brother, husband and the like, all at one time. This is possible because he is father from the point of view of his offsprings, son from the point of view of his parents, husband from the point of view of his wife and brother from the point of view of his brothers and sisters. Every attribute or adjective is therefore relative and not absolute. It depends upon our purpose or intention as to which of the several relationships is to be given prominence. Sometimes the role of a man as father may be more prominent when his rights and duties in respect of his children are being discussed; but when the duties of a citizen to pay tax to the government are being discussed, his role as a tax-payer and not as a father becomes prominent. If this is so, will it be correct to say that Mr. so and so is a father alone and none else ? This is obviously foolish as no body can be a father without being a son and a husband first. What best can be said about him is that he is father besides having so many other designations. The avoidance of insistence upon one aspect due to the recognition of the fact that there are several other aspects equally important is the underlying principle behind the philosophy-of-standpoints. Again, every thing in the world is subject to change which means emergence of one form and disappearance of another. But emergence and disappearance, these two terms refer only to the conditions of a substance and are not applicable to the substance itself which neither emerges anew nor disappears for ever but exists at all times. When the gold bar is melted and converted into an ornament, its previous form disappears and a new one emerges, gold remaining present in both the cases. If this is so, should we call things as momentary or everlasting ? According to the philosophy-of-standpoints things may be said to be momentary because they undergo a constant change in their appearance; and are also everlasting because they never perish and always exist in some form or the other. So it is a matter of a point of view as to what kind of statement about a certain object will hold good. One more difficulty arises when we attempt to describe things. All description is made through words which have several limitations. For example, the speaker and the listener must be conversant with the words used; and both the parties must think about the same thing in the same sense. Moreover, language has its own pitfalls. The most serious drawback of words is that they cannot catch up with the speed of change because by the time words are used, the object undergoes a further change. Because of these limitations of language all about a thing can not be fully described, there remains something undescribed, in spite of all saying, some thing remains unsaid. The philosophy-of-standpoints takes cognizance of this fact also. Thus a question may be answered in seven different ways. For example, you may ask me if I am a Rotarian. The obvious answer is No, because I am not enrolled as a formal member of the Rotary club. But if you consider that a person who firmly believes in the ideal of Rotary is a Rotarian, I may call myself to be a Rotarian. So I am a Rotarian but not a Rotarian. A fourth answer may be that it is indescribable. Fifth, it is indescribable that I am a Rotarian, Sixth, it is indescribable that I am not a Rotarian; Seventh, it is indescribable that I am a Rotarian but not a Rotarian.

Let us study the concept of Non-violence also. Violence may be physical, oral and mental. Jain religion prescribes that not only physical violence should be avoided, but a believer in the principle of non-violence should not hurt others by his words or should not entertain ill thoughts for injuring others. Further, violence may be actional, occupational, opponental and intentional. A man living in society can not altogether do away with violence arising out his normal activities of the day, violence arising due to his following an occupation, and violence arising out of his opponent's attacking him. But he can certainly avoid violence arising out of his intention to injure others. One should try to be non-violent in thoughts even if it is not possible for one to be able to be cent per cent non-violent in practice owing to one's circumstances.

All violence arises out of conflict and the conflict arises when due recognition is not given to others' point of view. It is by appreciation of others' standpoint and not by mere insistence on our own version of things that we may succeed in lying solid foundations on which may stand the superstructure of society's peace and prosperity.

Let us make a re-appraisal of religion and its relevance in the present day world. Jainism defines religion as a force which helps man attain his true self. Just as ignition may be called as the true-self of fire; flow of water; and cold of ice; knowledge and bliss of the highest order may be said to be the true self of the soul. The process by which the soul is enabled to find out its true attributes may therefore be called a religious process. Such a definition of religion leaves no scope for disagreement as the emphasis here is on the goal rather than on the different ways leading to it. Thus religion in its true perspective may be viewed as a purifying potent force which helps man to regain his true identity which has become obscure and opaque by numerous factors. In the interests of our individual and collective well-being we may do well by drawing sustenance from the life-giving recipes such as non-violence and the philosophy-of-standpoints. There is no doubt that for dispelling what is unjust and ignoble, mankind will have to imbibe qualities like tolerance and compassion and shall then be able to find out a lasting solution of the multifarious difficult problems it is now facing.

Let me conclude with a prayer which is sung as a part of daily worship in the Jain Temples—May all in the world be happy, may the administrator be upright and strong; may the rains be timely; may the diseases come to an end; may there be no famines and thefts; and may the righteous path lead all beings to progress and prosperity.

# Somadeva Suri and His Contribution to Jain Philosophy and Literature

**13**

*P. Chenna Reddy*

Jainism is one of the earliest religions of India. It is purely indigenous to India. It is a well established and fully developed religion. It was founded by twenty four *Tirthankaras* and the first *Tirthankara* is Rishabha. It is a religion based on the way of life preached and practised by *Jinas* (the word means the people who conquered their egos). It was a branch of neither Brahminism nor Buddhism. It actually emerged as an antithesis to Brahminism. Unlike the latter, it treats the people of all the castes equally. It welcomes even *śudras* and *avarnas* into its fold with open arms. It leads all the people irrespective of their caste to salvation. This universality appealed to the people very much and it flourished very well. It started in Andhra Pradesh long before Buddhism emerged in India. According to the tradition, Rishabha, the first Tirthankara, himself introduced it here. His first son, Bāhubali became the King of South India. He ruled it for a short time and renounced it to follow the austere path. He attained *siddhahood* at Podanapura now called Bodhan. He was succeeded by his son, Bharata, after whom India was named. He erected a colossal statue of his father at Bodhan.[1] According to *Haribhadriya Vritti*, Mahāveera himself came to Andhra to preach Jain faith.[2] It flourished here very well before the Mauryan dynasty started ruling India.[3] King Samprati, the grand son of Aśoka, not only became a Jain himself but also sent his missionaries to spread the message of Jainism in Andhra, Chola and Karnataka.[4] Jainism did not enjoy prosperity all the time in history. It saw many vicissitudes. It suffered great setbacks owing to the domination of Brahminism and Buddhism. The caste system of Brahminism infected Jainism and its presence was mentioned in several inscriptions and also attested by Somadeva in his *Yasastilaka.* The myths and folktales narrated in *Yasastilaka* are those of Brahminism. A special feature of Andhra Jainism is the worship of Jinas with milk and flowers.[5] Several great Jain saints endeavoured and strove greatly to rejuvenate Jainism at various times in history. Some kings patronised Jainism while others neglected it. Thus it suffered a setback during the reign of Satavahanas whereas it received good patronage in the hands of the Nolamba Pallavas and the Chalukyans of Vemulavada. King Baddiga II built a great Jaina temple and Arikesari IV, his own son, developed it later. It is during their period that Somadeva Suri, a great Jain philosopher and poet, lived and served Jainism greatly under their patronage.[6] He wrote several books on Jain philosophy and his *Yasastilaka* earned him great fame and reputation. The book is not only a good piece of literature in Sanskrit but also a good treatise on Jain philosophy and a great source of the history of his contemporary society.

The Chalukyans of Vemulavada were the vassals of the Rashtrakutas. Vemulavada (Karimnagar District in A.P.) was the capital of their kingdom. The Vemulavada Chiefs patronised Jainsim. The great Jain poets, Pampa and Somadeva, flourished in their courts. It is said that the chiefs built Subhadhama-Jinalaya.[8] According to the plates of Parbhani, Somadeva received from Arikesarin III, the nephew and successor of his late patron and was made the *sthānapati* of the temple in A.D. 966. The Jain monasteries of Vemulavada served as the great centres of learning where all the branches of knowledge were taught. The *Adipurana* and the *Yasastilaka,* major religious works of the time were written there. All the great religious and literary achievements of that period were due to the magnanimous patronage of these chiefs. Several great relics of Jainism such as the images of Tirthankaras can be found in Vemulavada even today. But unfortunately, this great centre of Jainism has become famous as an important Shaiva centre.

Somadeva Suri was a great Jain author and theologian. He came to Vemulavada probably from North India, received the generous patronage of the Chalukyas of Vemulavada and settled there in A.D. 959.[9] According to his *Yasastilaka*, he was a member of *Deva-sangha* and a disciple of Yasodeva. But the Parbhani Plates contradict this and say that he was a disciple of Nemideva, a pupil of Somadeva, a great Jain sage of *Gauda-sangha*. He was the younger brother of Mahendradeva and earned many honourable title such as *Syadvadachalasimba* (the lion on the mountain of Syādvāda), *Tarkika-chakravartin* (the emperor of logicians), *Vadibha-panchanana* (a lion to the elephants of disputants), *Vakkalloka-Payonidhi* (an ocean of stormy eloquence) and *Kavikularaja* (the king of poets) according to the colophon of his *Nitivakyamrita*. He was held in great esteem not only his contemporaries such as Pushpadanta and Maunjarya Vedighanghala Bhatta but also many kings of his age. He wrote his famous work, *Yasastilaka*, in the same year when his patron was with Krishna III at Melpadi in Chittoor district.[10] He wrote several books such as *Nitivakyamrita, Shannavati Prakarana, Mahendra-malali-samjalpa* and *Yuktichintamani-sutra* including *Yasastilaka. Yasastilaka* and *Nitivakyamrita* are the only extant works. He composed *Yasodharacharita* and *Syadvadopanishad* in addition to several verses.

*Yasastilaka* depicts the pathetic story of Yasodhara so it is also known as *Yasodharamaharajacharita*. It is more than a mere story of a king. It is encyclopaedic, giving information on all the possible subjects. It shows his immense scholarship. He makes use of very ornate style abounding in figures of speech and alliteration. He records his contemporary events in it. It is, therefore, an indispensable aid to the historian of mediaeval India. Besides all these, he conveys Jain philosophy through the story in his work. He depicts how different people renounce the world under different conditions. The story[12] narrated to King Yasomathi by Sudatta conveys that a king who sacrifices a dough cock instead of a live one undergoes many births and great suffering in the hell. The violence in one's thoughts is as sinful as the real violence. Understanding this, Yasomathi gives up hunting, renounces the world and embraces Jain faith. King Yasorgha does it on seeing his grey hair and crowns Yasodhara, his son, on the suggestion of sage. Queen Kusumavali feels like observing non-violence and accepts Jain faith. Later, her children follow her. Being moved by the comely appearance and mellifluous talking of innocent children, Abhayaruchi and Achayamati, to be sacrificed on the occasion of Navami festival at the temple of Chandamali, King Maradatta at once embraced Jainism under Sage Sudatta.

*Yasastilaka* describes the way of life of Jains. Sage Sudatta always travelled away from such places as are crowded with people, plants and animals in order to avoid violence and harm to them. He also shunned the places of mundane activities to guard himself from the fascination of mundane life. Jains were naked and unwashed. According to their faith, nudity is the order of Nature and bathing is not necessary for spiritual life. They believe that nudity and tonsure help them face the world boldly. They beg for alms and eat while standing. They filter water with a piece of clean cloth in order to avoid killing tiny living beings through drinking and drink it. According to Somadeva, an individual has to pass through the fourteen stages to reach the goal of salvation. He calls this ladder of fourteen steps *gunasthanas*. He has to free himself from his worldly existence as early as possible. He has to invite voluntary death, called *sallekhana* (fasting unto death), by taking the permission of his teacher and worshipping five *paramesties*. The death of a monk is celebrated with great pomp. The place where the dead body of a monk is buried or burned is called *nisidhi*. There are several *nisidhis* in Andhra Pradesh.[13]

*Yasastilaka* discusses five kinds of Jain ascetics : *sanyasi, sravaka, sadhu, suri* and *samayadipaka*. An ardent monk is called *sanyāsi*. A *sravaka* is specialised in astrology, incantations, deciding omens and the right time for religious functions and medicine. A sadhu accomplishes religious austerities and observes the principles of *mula* and *uttara gunas.* A *suri* attains such a higher position as to guide and lead the people across the sea of life with enlightening knowledge. He is revered as God Himself. Somadeva is a *suri.* A *samayadipaka* is the supreme ascetic. He makes use of such of his great skills as his supreme knowledge, political faculties and his power of eloquence and logic. Somadeva pays accolades to Sudatta as a great Jain teacher in his book.

Somadeva says that the mutual relation and influence of one's *karma* and one's soul is that of the rust of iron and the nobillity of gold. *Karma,* the past deeds influencing the present, causes bondage and the type of bondage depends on the type of *karma.* Both good and bad deeds cause bondage that prevents one from attaining salvation. According to Kundakunda, good karma brings gold fetters while bad karma brings iron ones. Only non-attachment can free one from these fetters. This is the same as the religious philosophy of Brahaminism. However, Jainism offers a different solution, that is, the path of three jewels : right faith, right knowledge and right conduct through which one can attain salvation. Somadeva discusses these things elaborately. The right faith consists of two things : *pravritti* and *nivritti. Pravritti* implies one's striving for salvation while *nivritti* involves one's abstaining from mundane things. Both these apply equally well to both a saint and a householder. The right knowledge makes one free from ignorance, scepticism and blunder. And the right conduct involves arresting completely all the activities that make one acquire *karmas.* Somadeva discusses twenty five kinds of obstacles to the observance of these three jewels. They called *dragdoshas* consisting of three kinds of *mudhata,* eight kinds of *madas,* six kinds of *anayatanas* and eight kinds of *sumkas.*

Somadeva describes four kinds of qualities to develop and maintain *samyaktva* (the right faith). They are called *upaguha, sthitikara, prabhavana* and *vatsalya.*[14] The first quality, *upaguha,* aims at protecting the reputation of one's religion and this may involve hiding the flaws of one's religion in addition to cultivating such qualities forbearance, truthfulness, honesty, purity and mercy and observing austerities, self-restraint and charity. They have to conceal the follies and foibles of their fellow followers of their faith otherwise others may look down upon their faith. Their religion will not be polluted by the faults of the petty people as an ocean cannot be spoilt by the death of a small frog. *Sthitika* involves protecting the faith of their fellow-followers. There are various kinds of people with different kinds of abilities and virtues. Everyone of them has a role to pay in the religion. If anyone wavers in his faith, they should help him overcome his wavering and skepticism. *Prabhavan* implies strengthening the faith through observing various kinds of rituals and spreading knowledge. They build temples, install idols and perform worship for this purpose. *Vatsalya* enjoins them to be compassionate and affectionate to their fellow-followers of the faith. It consists of three aspects. They have to revere their teachers, fellow students, community, the ideal of self-restraint and the study of their scriptures. This is called *vinaya.* They have to serve the sick and the miserable with commitment and dedication. This is called *vayavrtya.* They have to possess a pure, honest and complete devotion for their Jinas, their distinguished teachers and Jain scriptures. This is called *bhakti.* The Right Faith is to be supported by the Right Knowledge and they together help one achieve the Right Conduct.

In his *Yasastilaka,* Somadeva describes the initiation of various people into Jainism and the ideal life of various Jain saints. He depicts with great reverence the life of Sudatta who inspired several people to embrace Jainism. He is not adamant and rigid in his views. He is very catholic and accepts the principles and practices of other religions as long as they do not interfere with the fundamental principles of Jainism. These principles are called *mulagunas* and there are eight *mulagunas :* abstaining from alcohol, meat, honey and the five great fruits such as udumbara, asvatta palasa and nayagrodha. He, then, talks about twelve *uttaragunas* (secondary principles) : five *anuvratas,* three *gunavratas* and four *siksavratas.* By practising *anuvratas* and *gunavratas,* even a householder becomes as great as an ascetic. The *anuvratas* involve the renunciation of injury, stealing, falsehood, lust and greed. *Gunavratas* are a kind of preparation in restraining mind from the external objects through the renunciation of such propensities as injury, greed and indulgence and also of all the accessories to *hiṁsa* or violence. They are three and are known as *digvrata, desivirativrata* and *anantadandavrata*. And the siksavratas are very hard to follow. They include *bhakti* (devotion), *prosadha* (ceremonial fating), the limited use of worldly things to sustain one's life and *dāna* (charity).

Regarding falsehood, one should always speak the truth and should never lie. However, Somadeva shows his flexible views in exempting one from telling the truth when it puts him or the other in a jeopardy. One can thus hide the truth to prevent the possible violence or injury to oneself and others. According to him, ahiṁsa (non-violence) is to be practised in thoughts, speech and deeds. So the absence of the idea of killing is as important as the abstention from killing. However, *sankalpa* (the motive) is more important than words and deeds. A householder can be ascetic by observing all religious principles even if he has a family and other attachments. Non-violence and compassion for all living beings (*ahiṁsa* and *jivadaya*) is the supreme principle that leads us to our salvation. The qualities that we must cultivate to practise *ahiṁsa* are *maitri* (amity), *pramoda* (bliss), *karunya* (mercy) and *madhyasthya* (moderation). In addition to all the above things, Somadeva obliges a Jain householder to observe six duties every day in his life. They are the worship of gods, the adoration of teachers, the study of scriptures (*svadhyaya*), the physical and mental activities for the purification of one's soul through the removal of both external and internal impurities (*tapas*), the control of passions (*samyama*), the observance of one's vows and charity (*dana*).

Somadeva is a great Jain poet and philosopher. He excels many in his poetry. He is catholic in his views and thus contributed to the propagation of Jainism greatly. He composed many salutations and hymns in ornate prose and poetry. They are very popular and used by Jains in worshipping Jinas. They form a major and commendable part of the devotional literature of Jainism. Though he wrote many books, only a few are available presently. His *Yasatilaka* is revered greatly in Jain literature as it serves as a good guide to Jains. It describes the fundamental principles of Jainism through various tales, legends and anecdotes. It is a *champu kāvya,* a very good piece of literature written in prose and poetry. It helped historians greatly in knowing his contemporary history. It earned Somadeva great fame and made him immortal.

## References

1. Epigraphia Carnatica II, 234, (85).
2. *Haribhadriya Vritti,* Agamodaya Sammithi, 218-220.
3. Epigraphia Indica XXI, 71-89.
4. Indian Archaeology XI, 246.
5. P. Arundhati, *Brahminism, Jainism and Buddhism in Andhra Desa* (Delhi : Sundeep Prakashan, 1990) 294.
6. S.G. Murthy, *Jain Vestiges in Andhra* (Hyderabad : 1963) 55-56.
7. Somadeva, *Yasastilaka,* Trans. Handique (Sholapur).
8. N. Venkataramanayya, *The Chalukyas of Vemulavada* (Hyderabad : 1953) 45.
9. N. Venkataramanayya, 46.
10. Ibid. 47.
11. G. Jawaharlal, *Jainism in Andhra* (Jaipur : Prakrita Bharati Academy, 1994) 125.
12. Girish Karnad wrote *Hittina Hunja,* a play, in Kannada, basing on this story.
13. P.B. Desai, *South Indian Jainism* (Bhargava) 246-49.
14. Handique, 261-62.

# The Eternal Message of Jain Wisdom

14

*D. C. Jain*

The stream of knowledge has been incessantly flowing in India since times immemorial and credit for this goes to the seers, saints and Tīrthaṅkaras, who have guided and inspired mankind to tread the sublime path of righteousness in order to realise the truth.

## Jaina Tradition

Jainism is one of the oldest religious traditions of the world. Jaina scholars trace its origin back through almost limiteless time. The present historians, however, say that it is at least 5000 years old. A great generation of Tīrthaṅkaras, Āchāryas, saints and scholars belonged to this tradition. Lord Mahāveera was twenty-fourth Tīrthaṅkara of the present era. He was not the founder of Jainism but was propounder of this great religion. He realised his true self and attained omniscience by practising rigorous austerities and penances. A glimpse into his life shows that he was an embodiment of non-violence and compassion. Although Mahāveera (599 B.C.-527 B.C.), preached 2500 years ago, his preachings are relevant even today and bear special significance for the spiritual advancement of mankind. His message is full of pragmatic optimism, self-reliance, self-discipline and self-purification to develop inherent and infinite potentialities of human self.

## Contribution of Jaina Faith

The contribution of Jaina faith to Indian thought and life has been very significant. Actually, vegetarianism, as a habit prevailing throughout the Indian continent, practised by a large majority is an evidence of Jaina influence. Indian art, literature, architecture, painting and sculpture as also every other aspect of life have been greatly influenced by Jaina thoughts. Jainas are noted for the catholicity of their outlook and broad mindedness. The other significant contribution of Jainism is its harmonious and peaceful approach to life. The central themes of the teachings of Lord Mahāveera are non-violence, non-absolutism and non-possession.

## Non-violence

Non-violence is equality of all living creatures. If you feel that every soul is independent and autonomous, you will never trample on its right to live. This leads you to compassion and kindness towards all living beings and results in harmony and peace in the world. The principle of non-violence in Jainism embraces not only human beings but also animals, birds, plants, vegetables and creatures in earth, air and water. It is the holy law of compassion extended to body, mind and speech of a living being. Lord Mahāveera says, "All living beings desire to live. They detest sorrow and death and desire a long and happy life. Hence one should not inflict pain on any creature, nor have any feeling of antipathy or enmity. One should be friendly towards all creatures (Āchārāṅga Sūtra, 1.2.3.4.)."

## Positive Aspect of Non-violence

The positive side of non-violence is as important as the negative side but it is sometimes not fully appreciated. The positive aspect implies forgiveness, kindness, charity and service. This has been beautifully explained in a verse by the renowned Āchārya Amitagati of the 11th century A.D. as follows :

Satveṣu maitrī guṇiṣu pramodaṁ
kliṣṭesu jīveṣu kṛpāparatvaṁ

mādhyasthabhāvaṁ viparītvṛttu
sadā mamātma vidadhātu deva!

— Sāmāyika Pāṭha, 1

i.e., friendship towards all beings, respect for the qualities of virtuous people, utmost compassion for the afflicted beings and equanimity towards those who are not well disposed towards me–may my soul have these dispositions for ever.

## The Other Vows

All the other vows preached in Jainism are only an extension of the vow of non-violence. Truthfulness is essential to keep order and harmony in society. There are moments in life when one has to work hard to keep up one's convictions. In business and in our day-to-day dealings our truthfulness is put to test. We have to practise it constantly to maintain our integrity. While observing the vow of non-stealing, one is required to earn his livelihood by honest means. We violate the vow of Aprigraha by accepting and holding what is not needed by us. What we possess in surplus has to go to those who need it badly. The principle of continence is significant in maintaining the morals in society.

Thus we see that these principles, preached by Lord Mahāveera, are universal in character and are applicable to every individual in any society. These simple rules can be practised without the least philosophical speculation, even by an ordinary man.

## Integral View of Life

Jainism takes an integral view of life. Either faith or only knowledge by itself cannot take us to the path of salvation. We should have a combination of right faith, right knowledge and right conduct to tread the path of salvation. These constitute the three jewels of Jainism. Without right faith, there is no right knowledge and without right knowledge there is no virtuous conduct. Lord Mahāveera says, "By knowledge one understands the nature of substances, by faith one believes in them, by conduct one puts an end to the flow of karmas and by austerity one attains purity". (Uttarādhyayana Sūtra, 28.35)

## Concept of Karma

The significant achievement of Tīrthaṅkara Mahāvīra's revolution in spiritual field was the upholding of the concept of karma in place of the creator God. He said that man is the architect of his own destiny and he can rise only by his own efforts and not by the grace of any external agency. God is devoid of attachment, hence there is no need for him to create this universe, which is beginningless and endless.

Every inexplicable event in the life of an individual occurs due to the karmas accumulated in his previous birth. Karma is conceived as something essentially material which gets interlinked with immaterial soul. As particles of dust get attached to the body smeared with oil, so does karma with the soul. Lord Mahāvīra says, "Attachment and aversion are the root causes of karma and karma originates from infatuation; karma is the root cause of birth and death and these (birth and death) are said to be the source of misery (Utt. Sū., 32.7). He further add, "None can escape the effect of their own past karmas". (Utta. Sū., 4.3).

## Conquest of Passions

Lord Mahāvīra was a great believer in soul, godliness, karma and rebirth. According to him, a man should lift his soul by his own efforts. He says, "The soul is the begetter of both happiness and sorrow; it is its own friend when it treads the path of righteousness and is its own enemy when it treads the forbidden path" (Utta. Sū., 20.37). The prerequisite to the path of righteousness is to conquer the four passions, viz., anger, pride, deceit and greed and the five sense-organs. He says, "Conquer anger by forgiveness, pride by humility, deceit by straightforwardness and greed by contentment" (Daśavaikālika Sū., 8.39). According to Mahāvīra, conquering one's own self is the most difficult thing. He never ignored this aspect in his preaching. He says, "Victory over one's self is greater than conquering thousands and thousands of enemies on the battle-field. A true conqueror is one who conquers his own self (Utta. Sū., 9.34).

## Futility of Material Comforts

Lord Mahāvīra says that all material comforts and pleasures can never satiate anybody and give him true happiness. He preached the doctrine of non-possession to limit the desires for worldly pursuits. He says, "It is owing to attachment that a person commits violence, utters lies, commits theft, indulges in sex and develops a yearning for unlimited hoardings (Bhakta-Parijñā132). Possessiveness and greed are the main causes which create tension in the life of an individual and also in the society at large. Hence, as aspirant should limit his possessions and desires to the minimum extent.

## Equality

Mahāvīra laid great stress on the equality of all human beings. Stressing action and not birth as a determining factor of superiority was a radical step in the teachings of Mahāvīra. He proclaimed, "A person does not become a monk by merely tonsuring, nor a Brāhamaṇa by reciting the Oṅkāra Mantra, nor a Muni by living in the forest, nor a hermit by wearing clothes woven out of Kuśa grass. One becomes a monk by equanimity, a Brāhmaṇa by celibacy, a Muni by his knowledge and a hermit by his austerities" (Utta. Sū, 25. 31, 32). He boldly condemned the caste system based on birth alone for the defects that had crept in it at that time.

Lord Mahāvīra had great regard for women. He said that both men and women were eligible to attain emancipation after destroying the passions and karmas. He declared, "There are many virtuous women who are famous for their purity and chastity. They are like the goddesses before whom even the celestials bow" (Bhagavatī Ārādhanā 995).

## Importance of Human Effort

The importance of human effort is emphasised by Mahāvira which rules supreme in Jainism. He asserts in Uttarādhyayana Sūtra, "This life is most difficult to obtain. Just as the dry leaves of a tree wither away, so also when duration of life terminates human life too comes to an end (Utta. Sū., 10. 1). It is only the ignorant who do cruel acts and hence are tied to the cycle of birth and death. In Daśavaikālika Sūtra it is said, "One should endeavour on the path of righteousness before old age creeps up, the senses become feeble and man falls prey to all kinds of diseases" (Daśa. Sū.,. 8.36).

Dharma preached by Mahāvira is called Vitarāga Dharma. He himself practised it first and then preached the same to others. In religion, internal purity is more important than external observance. Lord Mahāvira says in Uttarādhyayana Sūtra, "The path of salvation really rests in insight, critical knowledge and pure conduct; clothes and other religious paraphernalia are just outside symbols". It has been repeatedly declared by both Śvetāmbara and Digambara Āgamas that "Even if an ascetic walks about unclad, grows lean and eats only once after months of rigorous fasting, if filled with deceit, he will be born endless number of times" (Sūtrakṛtāṅga Sūtra 1.2.1.9.)

## Catholicity of Approach

There has been catholicity and absence of dogmatic approach in Jaina belief. Lord Mahāvira said that Dharma is of prime importance to every one in life. In Daśavaikālika Sūtra, he says that righteousness (Dharma) is supremely auspicious. Its constituents are non-violence, self-restraint and austerity. Even the celestials rever him who is rooted in Dharma (Daśa. Sū. 1.1.) Any person, irrespective of caste, creed and colour can follow this path of purification.

## Ethical Code of Conduct

Jaina scriptures describe the conduct elaborately, expected from a monk as well as a house-holder. The monk and nuns observe the five great vows (Mahāvratas) and the laity five primary vows (Aṇuvratas). The five Mahāvratas are total abstinence from violence, falsehood, stealing, sexual indulgence and possessions. This four-fold congregation known as Dharma Tīrtha (centre of worship) is still observed and proves that Jainism is a living religion. There are numerous monks and nuns and nearly ten million house-holders continuing the tradition, following virtually the same path as prescribed by Jinas. Jaina monks and nuns move about in all parts of the country bare-footed, keeping minimum equipment required for their spiritual practice. There are some Digambara monks too who remain unclad. Jaina laity still practise complete vegetarianism and mostly lead a life free of vices and intoxicants. At the same time, the Jaina community is richly endowed with education and material comforts. They lead in the field of industry and business and have established a large number of charitable institutions for the cause of education, medical benefits and service to the downtrodden.

## Heritage of Jaina Scriptures

The teachings of Lord Mahāvīra are preserved in Jaina scriptures, which have come down to us through a very rich tradition. the Tīrthaṅkaras preached and the Gaṇadharas gave a structure to those preachings in the Āgamas. The Āchāryas and the saints protected and preserved them. These Āgamas serve as the source of understanding Jaina philosophy and culture and also of Indian thought and way of life at that time. Mahāvīra's preachings are like the innumerable pearls of wisdom that are found in abundance in the limitless and unfathomable ocean of knowledge. In the words of the Late Upādhyāya Amarmuni, "The Sūtra literature of Jainas is deeper than the deepest ocean in which innumerable divine pearls of wisdom are hidden. It is a great store-house of golden words. It is important not only for the inspiration it gives to tread the path of righteousness and spirituality but also for the message it gives for the harmonious development of family and social life. The aphorisms on moral and ethical progress are scattered here and there in all the Āgamas, which lay a strong foundation for a peaceful and humanitarian world (Sūkti Triveṇī, p. 11).

# Śravaṇabelagola : A World-famous Jain Shrine

15

*C. M. Agrawal*

Followers of almost all the major and minor religions world-over cherish great reverence for the places where the divine souls of their respective religions were born, practised penance delivered sermons and attained deliverance. Besides, such sites are the representative of the archaeological, mythological, historical and cultural heritage of a country they belong to. They are as such termed the life and blood of the country. These places have become *tirtha* where pious spiritual acts are performed by the religious minded people for their own as well as that of human beings at large.

Such places have great importance in our country also and they have greatly influenced our culture. Jainism, like Hinduism and Buddhism and other sects has gone a long way in making its contribution to India's cultural heritage. Though not one of the oldest living religions of the world yet it is rooted in the Indian soil.

Mainly the two characteristic features which clearly mark Jainism out from all other religious system are firstly extreme tenderness shown towards all animal life and secondly the saint worship. This attaches great importance to the *Tirthankara* whose statues they regard superior to that of gods.

Affluent Jains are seen liberally contributing in different ways not only for the propagation of the own religion but also have constructed by their liberal donation huge and elegant *dharmśalās*, hospitals, schools and charity houses for the people of all castes, creeds and countries.

Śravaṇabelagola is one of the most important Jain shrines in India. Unshakable faith of the Jains in it has been drawing every day hundreds of people for several generations. It is nearly eight miles south of Chennarāyapatna in the Chennarāpatna Taluk of Hassan district of Karnataka. It is situated amidst exquisite natural surroundings between two hills-Chandragiri and Indragiri. It stands up boldly from the plain covered with huge boulders. It is a religious, historic and picturesque place. According to a tradition, Śravaṇabelagola is the place where Emperor Chandragupta had spent his last days after relinquishing his throne.

Though there are several Jain temples and idols at Śravaṇabelagola, yet the 58 feet tall naked statue of Gomateśwara, Bāhubali, situated an the Indragiri hill is the main attraction of the people. It is a colossal statue and is visible from miles around it.

Śravaṇabelagola, white pond of the *Śravaṇa* (Jain monk) is named after the colossal Jain image of Bāhubali and its prefix *Śravaṇa* distinguishes it from other *Belagolās*. The word *Belagola* is derived from the two Kannada words *Bela* (white) and *Kola* (pond) which allude to the beautiful pond in the middle of the village. Sanskrit equivalents *Śweta- Sarovara, Dhavala sarovara* and *Dhavala-saras* used in the inscriptions support this derivation. Some inscriptions mention the name of the place as Belugula and Belagula. It is also derived from a plant, white *gulla*. It alludes to a tradition that a pious old woman annointed the image of Bāhubali with the milk brought by her in a *gullakāyi* or gulla fruit in some epigraphs. The place is also designated as *Dēvara Belagola* (Belagola of the God) and *Gommata Pura* (the city of Gommata). Further, the epithet *Dakśinkāśi* (Southern Kāsi) is applied to it in some modern records.

The image of Gommateśvara stands on the summit of the Indragiri in an open court surrounded by a bottlemented veranda enshrining images of Jain saints. This enclosure is again surrounded by a large heavy wall mostly formed by boulders in their natural position.

According to a tradition Gommata was the son of Purudeva, the first *tirthankara* and the younger brother of Bharata; his name was Bāhubali or Bhiujabali. In a struggle for the empire between the brothers Bāhubali won but having regard for the elder brother as well as detachment from the worldly pleasures and glamours, handed over the kingdom of the earth to his defeated elder brother and himself retired from the world in order to practise penance. He thus became a *Kevali* and attained eminence by his victory over *Karma*. Bharata erected at Pandanapura his image. In course of time the region around the image became infested with innumerable *kukkutos, sarpas* or *cockatrices*. It afterwards became invisible to all except the initiated. When Chamunda Kāya heard of it, he set out to see it. But when he started on his mission, he found that the journey was so difficult that it was beyond his power to proceed. He resolved to erect such an image at Śravaṇabelagola. An arrow shot by him from Chandragiri struck a boulder on Indragiri in such a way that it appeared to him in the form of Gommata Chamunda Raya succeeded in getting this statue made with great efforts under the supervision of the monk Ariśtanemi. Though all the literary works support this tradition yet they differ in minor details.

A thorough study of the available inscriptions makes it clear that the statue of Gommata was erected by Chamunda Raya, the minister of the Ganga King Rajumalla Satyavākya or Rachamalla who reigned from 974 A.D. to 984 A.D. Since according to the tradition the consecration took place during the reign of Rajamalla, the statue must have been erected between the above two dates. But the *Chāmunda Raya Purāna,* a Kannada work composed in 978 A.D. by Chāmunda Raya in the long account it gives of the author's achievements, does not mention the erection of the statue. It is, therefore, reasonable to conclude that the image was set up after 978 A.D. In the absence of more precise information the date of the completion of the image may be taken as 983 A.D. The traditional date of the consecration of Gommata by Chāmunda

Raya, given in several literary works, however is Sunday, the fifth lunar day of the bright fortnight of Chaitra corresponding to 1028 A.D. The beautiful and natural colossal nude image of Gommateśvara stands erect on the summit of the large hill faces north. The shoulders of the image are broad and the arms hang straight down the sides, thumbs turned outwards. The waist is slender. From the knee downwards, the legs are short and thick. The figure has no support above the thighs. Upto that point it is represented as surrounded by ant hills from which emerge serpents and a creeper (Mādhavī) twines itself round both the legs and arms and terminates at the upper part of the arm in a cluster of berries or flowers. The pedestal represents an open lotus. The image is carved in fine-grained light grey granite and is bright and clean as if it had just been chiselled by an artist. It seems that this image was cut out of a huge granite mass which stood on the spot from beforehand as it was impossible to transport such a huge piece up the oval hill-side. The statue of Gommata on account of its position and size is extremely impressive. It is the biggest one among other monolith statues in the world.

It would not be out of place here to mention that two more colossal images of Gommata, though smaller than that of Śravaṇabelagola, exist in south Canara district; one at Kārkala and the other at Enūr. The image of Kārkala was erected in 1432 A.D. by Virapāndya. It is 41 feet 5 inches tall. The second at Enūr was erected in 1604 A.D. by Timmarāja of the family of Chāmunda Raya at the instance of Chārukirtti Pandita of Belgola. It is 35 feet high. Though these two images are identical with the Śravaṇabelagola statue in the way they are represented, yet they differ considerably in the delineation of the features. Besides these two, there is also a soap-stone image of Gommateśvara. It is about 20 feet tall and is situated at Bastihalli on the left bank of the Krishnarājasāgara reservoir of the Krishnarājanagara taluka. This was perhaps erected during the reign of Viśnuvardhan, a Hoysala King, by his famous general Punisamayya. Apart from this, at Śravanagutta near Mysore, there is also another statue of Gommata, 20 feet high on the top of a small rocky hill. A creeper twines round the thighs and arms as in other images while a cobra with expanded hood forms a support for each hand. In the absence of inscriptional evidences it is not found when or by whom it was erected.

The above description clearly shows that the statue of Gommateśvara at Śravaṇabelagola is not only the oldest but it is also the largest and the most beautiful of all the Gommata images found in Karnataka.

The Gommateśwar image at Śravaṇabelagola is undoubtedly a very beautiful as well as marvellous piece of sculpture in which the craftsmanship of the artisans is praiseworthy and their labour astonishing. The most remarkable is its free contemplative expression combined with a benign smile with which it looks at the people struggling for worldly pleasures. It fully symbolises the spirit of Jain renunciation of this worldly pleasure and the nudity of the image indicates total non-possession (Aparigraha). Its stiff and erect posture suggests perfect self control. The benign smile on the face shows his bliss and sympathy for the suffering names. Though there are slight anatomical short-comings, yet the image appears majestic and impressive. Famous archaeologist Fergusson says, "Nothing grander or more imposing exists anywhere out of Egypt and even there no known statue surpasses it in height." Several poets wrote beautiful poems in Kannada in the praises of this majestic, beautiful and great image. From the terrace around the Gommata image one can see the wonderful sight on all the four directions which extends our more than a radius of about forty miles. We, with the help of field glass can identify several famous places on a clear day from this very spot. Moreover, this has our indescribable charm at dawn, at sunset, in moonlight and in the darkness of a starlit night.

Besides, each and every deity or idol, worshipped there due to its peculiar nature has some special form of worship. So it is very important to know the methods and rituals while worshipping a deity or statue. The knowledge of the necessary items required during its performance has also a great relevance.

For quite a large number of people, especially the Jains, Śravaṇabelagola's main attraction lies in the *Mahāmastakābhiśeka* or the head-annointing ceremony. It is performed on a grand scale every twelfth year. The expenditure incurred in its celebration is also very huge and is partially met out by donations from the rich and partially by other agencies. The available sources record that the earliest *Mahāmastakābhiśeka* ceremony was organised in 1398 A.D. and the latest in 1993 in which the then President of India Dr. Shankar Dayal Sharma visited the famous shrine of Śravaṇabelagola and received the blessings of Gommateśwar. On this festive occasion to have a glimpse of this renowned celebration, countless pilgrims including women and girls, gathered here not only from the different parts of India but also from the world over. They are extremely enthusiastic to ascend the hill even before dawn so that they secure good seats for themselves enabling them to see everything conveniently. Among the devotees there are a large number of people who carried with them either brass or earthen pots. Much before the ceremony started all the available space in the temple enclosure was fully packed. Opposite the idol an extensive area was strewn with bright yellow paddy on which a good number of gaily painted earthenware pots, filled with sacred water, covered with coconuts and adorned with mango leaves were placed. Above the image there was elevated platform, on which stand several priests, each of them containing in his hand a pot filled with ghee, milk and other essential items. When the chief priest indicated, the contents of these vessels were poured simultaneously over the head of the idol. This ritual is known as the preliminary bath of Gommateśvar. After it the great bath of the idol took place. Amidst the great of several instruments, thousand pots were lifted from the reserved area to the platform and all their contents were poured down over the image. The priests chanted texts from the sacred books during this event.

Visitors feel highly elated to see it as this religious ceremony is not only attractive but its performances look like magical events. People gathered there cry '*Jai-Jai Mahārāja*'. The exclamations of the devotees indicates the acceptance of their offerings and prayers by the idols.

In the last and final annointing, fifteen different substances are required namely, water, coconut meal, plantains, jaggery, ghee, sugar, almonds, dates, poppy seeds, milk, curd, sandal, gold flowers, silver flowers and silver coins.

On both sides of the statue of Gommata, a little to the front, there were two *Chāmara* bearers. They were beautifully carved and richly decorated and ornamented. The right statue is that of a male *yakśa* and the left that of a *yakśiṇi*. There is a circular stone basin called *Lalita Sarovara* (the lovely pond) to the left of the colossus, the name being engraved on the ant-hill opposite to it, which received the water used in annointing the image. Near the left foot of Gommata a scale measuring 3 feet 4 inches is engraved. There are inscriptions in old Kannada, Marathi and Tamil. These inscriptions state that Chāmunda Raya got the image made and that Ganga Raja got the *Suttālaya* or the surrounding buildings constructed.

The *mandapa* or (pillared hall) in front of Gommata is decorated with nine well-carved ceilings. Eight of them have figures of the *aśta-dikpālas* (regents of the eight directions), while the central one has in the middle a fine figure of Indra holding a *Kalaśa* (water vessel) for annointing Gommata. The ceilings are artistically executed and considering the material used (hard granite), the work acclaims credit of the sculptors. From the inscription in the central ceiling, it may be inferred that the hall was caused to be erected by the minister, Baladeva, in the early part of the 12th century.

The Kannada, Marathi and Tamil inscriptions engraved on either side of the image immediately below those of Chāmunda Raya state that the enclosure around Gommata was erected by Ganga Raja, the general of Viśnuvardhana Hoysala. The cloisters in this enclosure enshrine a large number of beautiful images of Tīrthankaras, Yakśinī, Kūśmāndinī and Bāhubali. Most of them belong to high class Hoysala art. Many of these images bear votive inscriptions on their pedestals and there are name boards fixed over these images.

On account of its uniqueness, this is not only a place of attraction for the Jains only, but for its grandeur and sculptural magnificence and beauty it attracts visitors from world over. They come here and after seeing it are so filled with admiration that they stand wonder-struck at the sight of such a marvellous and, unrivalled place in the world.

Thus Śravaṇabelagola is a noteworthy place of pilgrim of the Jains. It is well connected with roads and railways. It is really unique in the world. During the period of every annointing ceremony this small village looks like a mini city. Besides, its being an important Jain shrine has also mythological, historical, cultural and architectural importance.

# Jainism and the Problem of Identity

16

*M.,P. Chaurasia*

In recent past, psychologists and sociologists have created the role of identity in individual's lives and in the dynamics of communities. Problems regarding the issue of identity are major causes of human conflicts and violence. Identity has been an important theme in religion and Jainism, even today it is a living religion. We shall see how Jainism tackles this question.

Identity implies both similarities and differences. It is like Hegel's identity in contradictions. An individual's identity– includes the similarity of individual to other individuals in many ways, as for example, same gender, occupation and race and at the same time, many differences from other individual, as for example, in gender, occupation and race etc. Identity has also a sense of continuity over time-a sense of being at one with oneself, as one goes through the different stages of life.

Each individual man has several foci of identity. As for example, a man belongs to Bihar may be a gent by gender, a Hindu by religion, a lawyer by profession, a liberal in his outlook, a BJP man in his political affiliation, a rich man in his economic status, a member of an aristocratic family by birth, and so on. And every foci of identity has its own place in the total picture of the individual's identity.

But some times identity not only helps the individual, rather over grown focus of identity harms the person in real sense. For example, a man whose national identity is overgrown behaves as a superpatriot, neglecting his broader humanity. He may be eager to exploit or destroy other countries for adding power and glory to his own nation. Different ideologies often give special importance to a special focus of identity. In recent period, especially in Indian context, Islam and Sikhism overemphasizes the gender, separateness, organised religions often emphasise denominational or caste affiliations. This overgrowth of one part (castism in north India) at the cost of the whole is similar to cancer that will kill the society one day.

Like individuals, communities also have their identity, which in its turn has various foci of identification. Groups of human beings tend to behave as though they are a different species of animals, based on differences such as nationalities and religion. Erik Erikson, the famous psychoanalyst, called this phenomenon pseudo speciation instead of, "perceiving or accepting a human identity based on a common specieshood, different tribes and nations, creeds and classes (and perchance political parties) consider themselves to be the one chosen species and will, especially in times of crisis, sacrifice to this claim much of the knowledge, the logic and the ethics that are theirs."[1] N.S. Xavier considers human beings, aggressiveness as more dangerous than the animals. "In animals aggression within the same species is minimal, whereas the human race has shown high propensity for aggression within its members, pseudo speciation plays a major role in one group of human beings feeling rightful in exploiting or damaging another group."[2]

Undoubtedly identity can be an integrating force that brings closer the various aspects of the individual, unites individuals in community and establishes harmony between communities. Nationalism, for example, fosters unity between different communities of a country. But on the other hand, both over upliftment foci of identity in Individuals and pseudo speciation of communities cause disorder and disharmony. In this context, religion plays an important role on the integrating side of identity as well as on the destructive side.

No religion on the earth teaches us to disguise the other human beings rather it learns intolerance, brotherhood and sisterhood of people. Sociologist Hans Mol defined religions as 'sacralization of identity.' The healthy side of religion not only teaches the one specieshood of human kind, but also transcends that level and emphasizes the spiritual specialness of all human beings. This is opposite of the tendency for pseudo speciation. On the other hand, the fanatical (fundamentalistic) side of religion is probably the biggest cause for pseudo speciation. The religious wars going on in various parts of the world bear witness to this fact. Moreover, on an individual level, religious fanaticism causes an overgrowth of certain foci of identity such as gender, race, caste, etc. For example, fanatic moslems treat women badly, fanatic christian whites exploit Blacks without sense of guilt and fanatic upper caste Hindus mistreat untouchable with no fear of bad *Karma.*

Now we should see how identity issue is applicable to Jainism. In Jaina religion and philosophy, issue of identity has been solved on three scales; first on the metaphysical ground, the second on the logical ground and third on the religious ground. According to William Johnston, a noted catholic priest and Buddhist scholar, "All faiths are the same in their innermost qualities although each has its own external peculiarity or super structure. People who are superficial in their religious life identify with the external trappings rather than the deeper faith which transforms the individual for the better."[3] Jainism as a religion insists on universal identity of spiritually matured individuals which is a challenge to religious fanatics because Jainism regards all religions and opinions on an equal plane. Jainism teaches us that every individual possesses merits and demerits. If each individual lives in his destiny and limitation with a regard for other individual, this is the best identity of an individual. Same thing is true for community, nations, religions and other things.

Now we shall discuss Jaina's logic and show how Jainism in its logic tries to solve the riddle of identity. Jaina's logic is said *syādvāda.* Some scholar mentioned that the logic is the expression of doubt. An eminent author of Indian philosophy, Prof. M. Hiriyanna comments in the following manner. "The half-hearted character of the Jain inquiry is reflected in the seven-fold mode of predication (*saptabhangi*), which stops at giving us the several partial views together, without attempting to overcome the opposition in them by a proper synthesis. The reason for it, if it is not prejudice against Absolutism, is the desire to keep close to common-beliefs".[4] But such allegation is not true. Jain itself refuted the superstition and prejudice on many places. *Syādvāda* is based on his metaphysics. In metaphysics Jainism holds that the objects are of multiple characters and except a *Keval Jñāni* no other persons are capable to know the infinite characters of the object. So we shall always pass a partial judgement. This view has a similarity with William James and John Dewey's views that every statement has a truth claim. Even modern sciences accept the multidimensional aspects of object and they have invented only three dimensional looking of an object. So, absolute knowledge of a thing is not possible, this is the creed of Jaina logic. Dr. C. D. Sharma very boldly supported the theory. "The word 'Syat' is used here in the sense of the Relative and the correct translation of *Śyādvāda* is the theory of relativity of knowledge. Reality has infinite aspects which are all relative and we can know only some of these aspects. All our judgements, therefore are necessarily relative, conditional and limited."[5] *Śyādvāda* teaches us that our all statements have partial truth, so we should not insist on its absoluteness and so is the case with other people's Judgment. If all individuals agree to this view identity among the schclar will become very easy.

Such confusion emerges because of partial study of Jainism. If we go deep into the Jainism, we shall find that this system provides a lot of freedom to the individual and it is the duty of the individual to cut out a career for himself. Jainism does not compel individual to select its mandate rather this system is always ready to advise only in selecting so. All confusion regarding the Jainism is created by later Indian thinkers who were the opponents of Jaina. Kundakunda in his commentary has differentiated between empirical and ultimate truth in the following words, "*Vyavahāra* is empirically true and ultimately false, it is only the *Shuddhanaya,* the *Paramārtha* which is ultimately true".[6] Even another scholar like C.D. Sharma also agrees to this view in the following manner, "Vardhaman Mahāveera takes the place of the absolute and is identified with pure-self. He is beyond speech, senses and thought and is the indescribable pure consciousness undefiled by any impurity... No body would like to deny *Anekāntvāda* and *Syādvāda* provided they are legitimately restricted to the phenomenal only".[7] In this regard we can also notice the view of Āchārya Amṛtchand. He holds, "*Vyavahāra* should be valued as the only means to reach *Parmārtha,* but it should not be *treated as the end,* for *parmārtha* should not be *degraded to Vyavahāra*".[8] Āchārya Amṛt.chand further suggests that just as a baby needs the help of grown up in learning to wallk, similarly a man, who remains on the empirical plane, needs the empirical view, but as long as the individual arises higher, he perceives everything as a manifestation of consciousness and realises only the pure Consciousness".[9] I request reader to glance over, especially, on those lines which are italic, degraded to *vyavahāra',* treated as the end, remains only on the empirical plane, needs the empirical view, they will themselves refute the allegation that Jainism has a problem regarding the issue of identity.

Thus, in Jainism, there is also a scope of two level life, one is by gradual exercise of faith, conduct and knowledge man can easily attain the *parmārtha* and the second, one can happily opt for the empirical life. If some one glances over only *tirthankara,* then empirical life and the facts of empirical life are false. *Syādvād* is a logical theory but its implications are purely practical. It compels us to regard the views of others and co-operate to each other. It has a tolerable temperament to deal with the people and all these jewels are based on Syādvād. Jaina thinkers never condemned others' views and empirical life. It seems so because we do not want to have burden of deep analysis. If the teaching of Jainism is analysed in a proper way, we can see that even empirical identification of the individuals is at hand from the present scenario of worldly life.

The most burning problem of the twenty first century is environmental pollution. Indian Supreme Court in its judgment on 31.3.2000 expressed deep concern over the problem and advised the government to stop the steering of all the old buses of Delhi, because they ejaculate so much smoke in the atmosphere. The another problem of the day is increasing graph of the crime like—abortion, rape, murder, loot and *hiṁsā*. If you open the daily newspaper you will find more news regarding the above mentioned incidents. I think, the fundamental postulate of Jainism is life which is similar with recent bioethics. Bioethics accepts the goodness as the first principle and life as the second, because for the sake of goodness even life can be finished and the law of the land also sanctioned such action[10] if it is found justifiable. But Jainism goes one step forward and holds life as the first principle, because it is a metaphysical system and its ethics is based on metaphysics. This intention of Jainism also focuses more on ahiṁsā. The tradition of *ahiṁsā* is an old practice in India. Its roots are found in upaniśads and *Varnāshramdharma*".[11] In *Chhandogya* Upaniśad it is said, *Athayattapo dānamarjavamhinsā satyavachanamiti ta asya dakśiṇah.*[12] So, *ahiṁsā* is emhasised not only by Jaina but also by other thinkers of India, because this one tool is sufficient to stop all the anti-life activities of the society. Even the problem of self-identity is the achievement of modern era. It is growing with the growth of individualism and privite life.

Modern age, in many ways, has developed so many commodities to enjoy the physical life. Instrument like condom, medicines like antipregnancy pills and stimulative injections, means of entertainments like cinema, T.V. etc are the achievements of our age and these are even according to M.K. Gomathi, the fourth satanic for human life.[13] These things are responsible for the growth of individualism and corruption in recent life. Jainism has enough efficiency to check all these things.

Jainism teaches us the best system of life and to develop positive individuality. We shall see how Jainism is able to perform these tasks. Jaina-ethical teaching has a practical approach. Process of conduct of which portion is *ahiṁsā*, truth, *Asteya* and *Brahmacharya* are the mile stones of human life. *Brahmacharya* itself is sufficient to prevent the rape, or unethical sexual relationship. *Ahiṁsā* is a sharp weapon against the hunting of wild animals and crime. Truth and *asteya* together are very strong pravṛti to stop the corruption and other bad habits of human beings. For the purification of environment, Jainism insists on the good-habits of disposing the stool and urine in a lonely place because there are many diseases which break due to infection from stool and urine. Jainism is far old system of philosophy, even then the system is wholly consistent with modern medical science. Healthy individual can live only in a healthy environment. In this way Jainism laid stress on preservation of animals, forestation and disposing of waste in a lonely place and all these activities are the key of pollution free environment.

From the bioethical point of view Jainism divides human personality into three parts—mind, body and *Jīva* and Jaina thinkers way out the process of nourishing these three aspects of human life to produce balanced human personality. Here I want to discuss the process of cessation of passion that helps us to purify the soul. *Karma* takes the central place in Jaina teachings. *Karma* is the link between soul and matter and passion is the root of *Karma*. It is said that the nature of human mind wholly depends on the food taken by the man. A purely vegetarian man is seldom an injurious person. Jainism is fundamentally a vegetarian system as holds P.T. Raju, "Jainism is spiritual in its motive, believes in the reality of the spirit, accepts the validity of inference and it condemned all shedding of blood, preached non-injury to all living beings and advocated vegetarianism".[14] The passion of a vegetarian person must be non-injurious as thus he will not attract the flow of *Karamic* matter. The man who is in process of cessasing one's passion is in process of purifying the soul. Certain *Karmas* have been sanctioned and some actions are prohibited, and some actions are coerced by Jainism. If the individual avoided the prohibited and coerced action and performed only sanctioned he can win the world, because he will necessarily succeed to get the state of self-restrainment. Through self restrainment we can control the growing population and we will get success to save the earth from collapsing. In Gujarat water level has gone very deep and there is a high cry for water. Animals are dying.[15] Why ? Because we have committed certain provoking actions with nature. Jainism teaches us a lesson of live and believe. The system believes life in plant and everything of nature. A vegetarian and ahiṁsakman cannot unnecessary touch the nature because such person must be a tolerable man. A tolerable man can easily recognise the identity of other and he believes in mutual co-operation. He likes to identify with others. He knows that overgrown identity either of the individual or of the community or of religion, is dangerous to the humanity.

The ethical teaching of Jaina also tells us to be more and more self-cultured. Author, like S.K. Mitra comments that Jaina ethics is lacking in its social aspects, "The Jain virtues aim at self culture than at social service."[16] A prominent Jaina thinker Vidyananda's classification of the virtues in *Aṣṭasāhastrī* shows that Jaina-ethics is nearer to intuitionism. Jaina ethics does not believe in consequentialism rather it holds that rightousness and unrighteousness of an action depends not on the action but on the intention or *abhisandhi* of the agent. It is not sufficient that action resulting in happiness is right and unhappiness is wrong. According to this system even non-sentient objects which are incapable of morality can produce consequences of happiness or suffering. Hence morality and immorality do not arise merely from results of happiness or unhappiness but depend on subjective intention or *Abhisandhi* which is absent both in the non-sentient objects and the saint. *Abhisandhi* is nearer to C. L. Stevenson's attitude theory. He also believes that good partly depends on attitude.[17] If *Abhisandhi* is pure, it produces good actions and if it is impure, it produces bad actions. Now if a person whose intention is pure why he will not identify himself with others with self identity. If every people lives within his own range with his limitation and destiny, the issue of identity may be solved easily and when an egoistic man encroaches his limitation the consequence is fascism that swallows up the entire humanity. Now if a person possesses only pure attitude how he can harm others ? And how he can hamper the identity of other individuals or community or nations?

Now, in this context we shall consider the metaphysical status of the Jainism that how this system is able to establish world peace and pleasure and how it deals with the problem of identity. Jainism in its outset is materialistic because it does not believe either in God or in any supernatural existence but at the same time it differs from materialism on certain issues, due to its ethical teachings and spiritual approaches. *Tirthankar* or *Kevaljñani* or pure-self takes the central place in Jainism. He possesses certain infinite qualities that can be attained only after fulfilling certain processes. Jainism believes in pluralism or *Anenkāntavāda* that accepts the existence of many things and beings. According to this principle, things have many characters and they all are independent. Only *Kaivalyajñani* can know all the qualities of all the objects, living and non-living. *Pudgals* and spirit are separate and independent entities. Jainism believes in the plurality of soul and the plurality is real. The objects have positive and negative qualities and both the qualities live together in the object in harmony. Only pure self is able to know all the qualities of all the things and beings. Those qualities which are changeable are called modes and those which are eternal are called attributes. Substance and attributes are inseparable because attributes are the essence of the substance and the substance cannot remain without it. Reality is unity and difference viewed from the point of view of substance a thing is one and permanent and real, viewed from the point of view of the modes it is many and momentary and unreal.

In this way, according to Jainism, man is bound by time, density nature and Karma but he is free at a moment before starting the *karma.* It means man is free in choosing and deciding.

He is free in taking the judgement before doing and dependent in doing. He is confined after the moment of starting the Karma. But man has capacity to repulse all the repulsive factors. For this purpose man has to march from physical body to ethereal body, from empirical to subtle. *Saṁskāra* of Jainism is similar to the gene of modern science and according to Jainism near about sixty thousand commandments are marked on a gene. This gene is the *Guṇa Sūtra* of Jaina due to which there is difference between man to man and their nature. Gene is a constitutive component of the physical body, while *Karma* is the factor of subtle body. Electric body is also the part of our body, that is also subtle, but *Karma*-body is many times subtle even than it. It is more microcosmic and on its each aspect infinite scripts are marked. the entire description of *purūṣārtha* are written on it. Soul is the fundamental balancing force between gene and Karma body. All forces relay from soul. This is medial source whose function is to originate the continuity. Those functions of soul are *Puruśārtha* or subjectiveness, *virya* and flashing on the mind. All these come from the soul the balancing point and our destiny is to reach there. This is repulsion or projection. When consciousness arises life and journey start ahead.

The best way to achieve this goal is to live in present and not in future. We should exercise our effort to live with the present circumstances and feel much hope or fear towards future. We should live neither in past nor in future, but only in present. If we account our 24 hours routine we will find that most time we live either in past or in future and only two or three hours we live in present. To achieve the bliss should be the main motto of one's life but it is possible only in present life, not in future or past life. According to Jaina bliss is veiled by memory and imagination. These are the essential factors of social life, but human beings unnecessarily extended it so much that basic aim of life has been left behind. Ladder of climbing and getting down is the same but changing of muscles and nerves in both the process are not the same. Eyes are the same but their changes are different in weeping and laughing. Human beings should select only those memories and imagination which are helpful in living with present time. Journey from physical-body to subtle is called observation and this process occupied analysis and explanation. *Viveka Sūtra* holds that realization of soul is the highest goal of life and it could be possible only when we will be determined to change not only our attitude but also the direction of our life. At first step heart will change. Changing of heart will change the harmons and other chemicals of body and lastly all these will change the human conduct. Changed conduct will stop the flow of *pudgals* and from here and hereafter ahead journey towards soul will start. This journey will lead to ashes, the Karma and *Saṁskāra.*

Like Kierkegaard[19] Jaina also considers three stages of human life : Some are confined to sensation and they do not know or they have no knowledge. Some persons know but they have no sensation. Some are those, who have knowledge and sensation both. Unconscious things neither know nor feel. Sensation is the first stage and knowledge is the later stage. Sensation is lowest stage of consciousness. This is professional stage of life. We all live in this stage, but this is not the stage of conscious process.

Phase of pure knowledge is sensationless because sensation is the symptom of body and not of the soul. When we become bodyless, we lose the sensation of pleasure and pain. One who possesses knowledge and sensation both, he is at the stage of mental and rational development. In this stage there is the seed of conscious development. With the development of knowledge subjectivity becomes sensationless and the subject is able to enter into the stage of perfect consciousness. Stage of pure knowledge is the stage of seer or *Tīrthaṅkara.* Knower and knowledge are neither same nor different. It is called the stage of pure knowledge. There are two status of soul—Assent and refusal. To have pure knowledge is the stage of refusal, because knowledge is the nature of soul and in this situation no transition of any *vijātīya* element is possible. Sensation is the stage of acceptance in which the subject is related to the acceptance of external world. Stage of refusal is the stage of *nirjara* (abolition). Pure realization of consciousness is the situation of the realization of *saṁwara* (stopping). Gene and *pudgals* have infinite energy. *Jīva* possesses two powers acquiring capacity and active capacity. Gene transforms into body, body transforms into active power and active power originates conjunction, conjunction produces pride and pride generates *Karma*-bondage and this is the cycle. Hate, passion, anger are the modes of body not of soul. Āchārya Amṛtachand holds :

> *Bhedvigyānth siddhāh, Siddhā ye kilakechana*
> *Tasyaivabhavto baddhān, baddhaye kilakechana.*[20]

Only those are bounded with *Karma* who have no knowledge of differentiation. One who knows the difference of conscious and unconscious, he can easily project himself beyond the world.

Now I want to refute certain allegation labelled against Jaina's ethical teaching. Dr. Radhakrishnan has considered that there are some elements of rigorism in Jaina's ethics.[21] In the similar way S. K. Mitra finds lack of social aspect in it.[22] This allegation is very trivial because Jains believe in freedom and responsibility as well as he advocated to lead a natural life. If artificial and luxurious life is good then I have nothing to say. If life without passion and malice is good, Jaina's theory of action is unparallel. Several times Jainism repeated that passion and affection towards external object is the root cause of bondage and individual should reach at the balancing point of existence i.e. neutral stage through projection of oneself beyond passion and malice.[23] Many times Jaina's ethics hold that affection towards world and its things limited our freedom of judgement to act.[24] True judgement is based on the eternal nature of man and his isolation from *vijātiya* thought. When man judges with his experience and realization his self judgement is always correct.[25] Even Maxmuller agrees to the ethical teachings of Jainism when he holds that, "Man is his own friend, why you expect friendship of other."[26]

We can remember the teaching of Jaina in context of Marxism and recent scientific researches of the world. At the very beginning Jaina holds that this world is natural outcome and there is no creator of it. This is part of the sky and it is eternal.[27] Changes in the world is due to *Kāladravya* and nothing else. This system of Philosophy is a heritage for those Indians who think of materialism and modern science as the right path of life. No God is the master of this world, no metaphysical rules govern the world but it is human passion, malice and will. Modern medical science establishes that the personality of individual can be changed by changing his gene. Jainism much before believes in changing the *saṁskāra.* But in this age of corruption, smuggling and artificial life style who is ready to listen to the gospel of Mahāveera ? But at least men like me are proud of this teaching that it is scientific, logical and materialistic[28] in its outlook and it has capacity to guide the world. To see the above stand point of Jainism certain critiques have raised the problem of identity with Jainism. But a short glance over the metaphysical status of Jainism seems that the objection is wholly wrong. The allegation can be refuted into two ways : One by showing the status of *Tirthaṅkara* and the other by showing the importance of eternal qualities. Eternal qualities of individual's souls are infinite power, infinite faith, infinite knowledge and infinite bliss. One who possesses all these qualities devoid of modes is pure-self. A prominent commentator of Jainism Kundakunda holds that, "even knowledge, conduct and faith, the three jewels of Jainism, which are regarded by Umaswami (Umaswati) as the path of liberation, are true only from the empirical stand point; from the absolute stand point, there is neither knowledge nor conduct nor faith, because the ultimate knower is the pure-self".[29] This assertion of Kundakunda shows that the essence of Jainism is a state of neutrality where only pure bliss will remain. If a person is embodied with pure bliss he may take the central place to identify. The other way is the state of *Siddhaśeelā. Siddhaśeelā* is a state of Calm and Peace and only *Tirthaṅkara* can hold it. One who attains the state of Siddhaśeela becomes Tirthankara. He possesses all the four perfections. With His own perfection he guides the people to reach there. Every individual of this world can easily reach there if they sacrifice their modes which are not their essential qualities. *Siddhaśeelā* is not a place, it is a state of mind and soul. If a person commands his breath and has a perversion towards world, he can very easily enjoy the state. This is the absolute state that can establish peace and pleasure in the world. This is the perfect identity with complete freedom to the individuals, society, nations and mankind. Possibility of differences is not there because many persons can enjoy the state of *Siddhaśeelā* together.

## References


1. Erik Erikson, *Dimensions of New Identity,* (W.W. Norton and Company, New York, 1974), p. 28.
2. N.S. Xavier, "Gandhi and the issue of Identity", *Gandhi Marg,* December 1986, p. 521.
3. William Johnston, *The Inner Eye of Love* (Harper and Row, Sun Francisco 1978), p. 26.
4. M. Hiriyanna, *Outlines of Indian Philosophy,* pp. 172–73.
5. C.D. Sharma, *A critical survey of Indian Philosophy* (Motilal Banarsidass, Varanasi, Second Edition, 1964), p. 52.
6. Kundakunda, ववहारो भूयत्तहो भूयत्तहो देसिदोदु सुद्धणो, *समयसार*
7. Siddhasena's view, Tr. by Dr. C.D. Sharma, in *A critical Survey of Indian Philosophy,* p. 61.
8. Āchārya Amṛt Chand, *Commentary on Samaysara,* p. 20.
9. Ibid, p. 29, तदापि परमार्थम चिच्चामतकारमात्रम् पर विरहितंतह-पश्चताम् नैस किंचित।
10. For wide discussion See J.P. Thiroux, *Ethics : Theory and Practice* Especially, p. 144.
11. S. Radhakrishnan, *Hindu View of Life,* p. 117.
12. *Chhandogya,* 3/17. अथ यत्तोपोदानमार्जवमहिंसा सत्यवचनमिति त अस्य दक्षिणाह।
13. M.K. Gandhi, *Young India,* Part 3, p. 120.
14. P.T. Raju, *Introduction to Comparative Philosophy,* (Motilal Banarsidass, Delhi, 1992), P. 213.
15. *Hindustan* (Hindi) Daily Patna, 7.4.2000.
16. S.K. Mitra, *The Ethics of the Hindu* (Calcutta Univ. Press, 1963, p. 221.
17. C.L. Stevenson, *Ethics and Languages,* (Yale Univ. Press, 1945), p. 1 to 4 for wide discussion.
18. Umaswati, एको भावह सर्वथा येन दृष्टः सर्वे भावाह सर्वथा तेन दृष्टाह, गुण पर्यायिवाद द्रव्यम। तत्वार्थ सूत्र, 5, 37।
19. Kierkegaard, *Unscientific Post Script,* for wide discussion.
20. Āchārya Amṛt Chand, *Jain Darshan Men Karma Srota,*
    भेद विज्ञानतः सिद्धाः सिद्धा ये किलकेचना तस्या भावता बद्धा बद्धाये किलकेचना।

21. Dr. S. Radhakrishnan, *Indian Philosophy,* Vol. 1, p. 294.
22. S.K. Mitra, op. cit., p. 220-1
23. *Pañchastikāya Samaysāra* 115 and *Tattvartha Suura*, 1:11
24. Ibid, p. 163.
25. Ibid, p. 165.
26. Maxmullar, *The Sacred Books of the East,* vol-22, p. 33.
27. *Saman Sutta,* 651.
28. M.K. Fuskele, "Ek Mahan Virasat ki Sahmati men Utha Hath", Pramarsha, Sept., 1986, p. 920.
29. *Kundakunda,* ववहारेणु वदिस्सै णाणिस्स चरित्त दस्सणम णाणम नविणाणम न चरित्तम न दस्सणम जाणगो सुद्धो। *समयसार*

# Mahāveera : An Inborn Sādhaka

17

*Neeraj Kumar*

Normally people, even would be great souls are so much engrossed in worldly affairs that they seldom make efforts to adopt spiritual life which may lead to deliverance. It is only when some such situations arise that reveal the meaninglessness of this worldly life, they turn to spiritual life and succeed in attaining and become great men and supreme souls.

Even Buddha, who was to become a supreme soul, before leaving home was leading a princely life. It was the sight of an old man, an ill man and a dead man which made him realize at once the emptiness of the worldly pleasure. He left home and by practising penances became a supreme soul. Vālmiki was leading a life of a dacoit and wanderer, when convinced by Nārada of the selfishness and disloyalty of his family members became a devotee of Rāma and in the long run became a great sage. Tulsidāsa, devoted to his wife, followed her passionately to her father's place. When she badly rebuked him for his infatuation towards her and told him about the dirt and filth of her physical body and asked him to devote himself to Rāma he left the place and became a dedicated devotee of Rāma and a great saint. But Mahāveera, on the contrary, needed no such situation and advice. He was an inborn *sādhaka*, destined to be a supreme soul and a spiritual leader of lacs and crores of people leading them on the path of spirituality and liberation Mahāveera was a great spiritual *Sādhaka* of his epoch. In his preachings, we find peace and prosperity of

Mahatma Gandhi, equinimity of Karl Marx, Panchaśila of Nehru and fraternity of Guru Nanaka Dev. Indeed he was a great saint, preacher and divine guide and a ray of divine hope for the suffering world. In his search for the pure truth he, kicking off the worldly pleasures available to him followed that immortal path of *Sādhanā* which provided divine light to thousands and lacs of *Sādhakās*. About twenty five hundred years back, the Republic of Vaiśali situated in the eastern zone of India, was on the summit of prosperity. Referring to the happy and prosperous citizens of the republic, Lord Buddha had once said, "If you want to see gods, you can look at the citizens of Vaiśali." The King of Vaiśali in modern terminology the President, was Chetaka, who was the full national uncle of Lord Mahāveera.

Kshatriyakund was an outstanding suburb of Vaiśali. It was governed by Siddharth, the King of the Republic of Jñatri. His beloved wife was Triśalā. Mahāveera was their third issue. The family name of Mahāveera was Vardhmāna. Later on, in view of his actions, his names Vīra, Mahāveer and Sanmati etc. became prevalent among the general public. Nandi-vardhan was his elder brother and Sudarśanā his elder sister. Mahāveera's marriage was performed with princess Yashodā. Priyadarśanā was Mahāveera's only issue.

The first thirty years of Mahāveera's life were spent in the elysium of prosperity and majesty. The path of his journey of life was at every step strewn with flowers, there was no trace of thorns anywhere. There followed all around the spilling stream of unrivalled and pure love of his friends, subject and other affectionate persons. Each and every person can easily speculate how fine, delightful and splendid like a blooming and fragrant lotus the life of a prince can be from his childhood to youth.

From his very childhood Vardhamāna was highly venturous and fearless. Fear, apprehension and docility did not even touch him. He did not remain confined in his golden chambers full of all types of happiness and amenities. He liked to move here and there with free mind and play an occasionally arranged various types of sports and games. In the company of his loving associates and companions belonging to the poor and the rich families of his neighbourhood he visited forests lying outside the city and played there. Once while playing in a garden he picked up and threw away from the playground a dangerous black serpent. Other boys playing there getting panicky, started crying and there took place terrible stampede, but Vardhamāna stood absolutely fearless.

In the same way while he was once playing, a god adopting a highly dreadful form wanted to frighten Mahāveera. His playmates were frightened but Mahāveera, really a courageous boy could not be frightened. He, by his fearlessness and courage defeated that god, in the form of a demon. The stories of Mahāveera's courage, recorded in the pages of ancient epics, have been and shall ever be the source of inspiration, fearlessness, courage and valour in us.

For his education he was admitted in a famous *gurukula* of his time, but the atmosphere of the place could not satisfy him. Mahāveera's inquest was quite different, it could not be solved there. He had no interest in the education and initiation externally imposed from outside. He was such a powerful seed as in every field of development sprouts from within. He in his very childhood logically reconciled intricate doubts of Indra, the King of gods. This much is certain that Mahāveera possessed inherent genius. His mind was highly conscious. He could give proper solution to every complicated question. Whatever a youngman needs was available to him, golden throne, royal palace and a beautiful and loving wife. There were his relations who loved him more than their own life. Prosperity, happiness, cheers lay at his feet and he possessed fully healthy and strong body and mind. Then what was reason that in his full youth, renouncing every thing, he started all alone towards awful lonely forests, deep mountain caves and sky piercing mountain peaks ?

In man's personal life and also in the life of the people around us physical ailments—mental agony, birth, old age, death, casual troubles and rivalry are so powerful that no vigilant mind can help thinking about them. Many a time to get rid of them, paths are searched out, desired means of retaliation are gathered and for a few moments man also forgets himself in this maize but the hollowness and shallowness of these efforts each and every enlightened scholar can realise. Physical rest, for some moments, is definitely a means of giving freedom from instantaneous troubles but it is not a permanent solution. The real means of freedom from troubles is somewhat different.

Life has certain specific purpose. It is neither meant for being helplessly destroyed by pains and troubles arising from birth, old age, death, physical diseases and mental agonies, nor to stroll in the stinking lanes of desire for enjoyment of wordly pleasures. Life has some great purpose, without attaining which it is meaningless. Life full of the germs of perversions is no life at all. To attain passionless piety in life and the endless truth is the supreme purpose of life. Finding out the path of its fulfilment is compulsory for an enlightened and conscious *Sādhaka*. In the inner mind of Mahāveera there was a strong desire for this very thing. In his inner mind persisted the readiness to renounce everything for procuring it. He felt that such means as cannot give permanent and passionless bliss, then there is no sense in running after them with closed eyes. In the depth of whose hearts, strong desire to achieve the supreme truth and bliss is awakened they are not satisfied with superficial happiness and amenities. The erotic coquetry of the family, financial prosperity and the free means of enjoyment of worldly pleasures are not able to give eternal solution to the life in the direction of achieving the aim. If in a certain life there is no movement in this direction then that is nothing but a waylaid and vagabond life. In the absence of an aim, life gets cut into pieces. Aimlessness gives birth to meaninglessness and bewilderment. This position was quite obvious in the mind of Mahāveera.

Attainment of 'self' and 'search for the self based bliss' was the aim of Mahāveera. This was the motivation that compelled him to change his traditional path of life. This motivation he got neither from any other person nor from any so called religious preacher. The motivation had emerged from the depth of his own heart. This very innate internal motivation of Mahāveera is the basis of all his future attainments.

The reason behind Mahāvira renouncing home was not his indifference towards life. There was neither any family worry nor any social dissatisfaction, nor personal troubles nor mental depression. He was quite happy and free from mental and physical worries and also from that of his family and kingdom. He never had to face such a situation that inspite of his desiring he did not get his desired objects. In the name of happiness and prosperity there was available everything all around. Yet there was void inside. This void was not physical but spiritual. Inspite of the dazzling outside light, darkness lay hidden somewhere in his inner self. There was no other problem except this that his internal spring of bliss was obstructed. In the absence of this innate bliss every other thing was meaningless for him. This was not only Mahāveera's personal problem but that of the entire humanity.

Consciousness is one and indivisible so what is true for one is true for all and what is true for all is true for one. Contribution to the development of total humanity as well as individual is the lone attainment of a *tirthaṅkara*. In Mahāveera such an all round auspicious light was to shine. The main reason behind his leaving home was to awaken endless consciousness in respect of 'self' and 'other' and open the flood-gate for the stream of endless bliss. There is difference between 'doing' and 'being done'. In 'being done' is naturality non-obstinacy but in 'doing' there is a tinge of obstinacy and persistency. The process of *Sādhanā* followed by great *Sādhakas* is natural, innate and uncontested. So Mahāveera's renouncing home was natural and inner motivation. The main reason of his accepting ascetic life was his strong desire to endow the life of the common people with the stream of endless bliss.

The centre of spiritual practices in the soul has not special relations with external 'yes' or 'no'. Favourable or adverse external environment and the presence or absence of means in themselves are neither instrumental nor obstructive. The real artifices or obstructions exist inside us. All the spiritualists till now have been saying that when the ray of knowledge is to shine, it shines anywhere. For it there is no restriction of this or that place. There is not only a single example of Bharat, we get hundreds of such examples in Indian literature. But there is no dearth of contrary examples also. Innumerable great *Sādhakās* going to lonely and peaceful environment of the forest, have performed penances. From the point of view of religious practices such an environment is more suitable than that of home. The *Sādhaka* is free from disturbances and distractions and also alluring homely comforts and amenities. And when he receives reproof and insult from all corners then he really gets an opportunity to test his equanimity, forbearance and fortitude.

Not only one but both the courses are true. Every *Sādhaka* has his own condition. So there can be no single definite course for both the types of the *Sādhakās*. For some *Sādhakās* lonely and peaceful forests is good. In such a place it is easy to concentrate one's mind. So ordinary *Sādhakās* in their search for the truth go to lonely and peaceful places. Mahāveera also followed this course and got success in his mission. But lonely environment is not an essential constituent of concentration leading to the attainment of the real form of the self. Sometimes an inadvertent *Sādhaka* also on account of his insistence on loneliness goes astray. And sometimes such *Sādhakās* also as living in home and insisting on getting everything gets nothing. The real thing is the promptitude of mind. Both the courses in different contexts, reveal the same truth.

There is one thing more which is a subject of discussion in respect of a *Sādhaka*. Such discussion arises in the case of Mahāveera also. Why should one leave home and keep himself away from the responsibilities of his family ? These are the questions which are often being asked in respect of home renouncing *Sādhakās*. A few arrogant persons name even Mahāveera as coward. But it is not proper to think or say so. Mahāveera was not a coward who shirked his responsibilities. The responsibility of the family, husband and wife and children has importance only upto a particular limit. In life sometimes come such important occasions when the petty limits of responsibility break away of their own accord. A brave warrior who for the defence of his country dies fighting in the battlefield or a youngman who fighting against injustice and atrocities lays down his life are not cowards. To give up the infatuation for the family, beloved wife and innocent children and to adopt the difficult path of conflicts for the sake of a great ideal and to kick off the available pleasures and amenities and to bear hard and dreadful calamities is not cowardice, but bravery and such brave men as make sacrifices are counted and rare in the pages of history. Mahāveera, the searcher of the truth, was really such a lustrous and brave man. At the age of thirty in his full youth when the eyes of young man are hardly found open, to renounce the golden throne of prosperity and worldly pleasures is really a herculian feat. When the voice of the inner truth starts calling anyone to do something then the petty calculations of domestic responsibilities fail to hinder his path. Neither tears resulting from passions nor the scorching words of bitter criticism can stop a true searcher from reaching his destination. On such occasions usually domestic and social responsibilities are undoubtedly neglected and the walls of traditional boundaries fall down. Mahāveera also was not an exception to it. In his heart, such a flame of truth arose as in it all his attachment for enjoyment of personal pleasures and infatuation for the family were burnt down to ashes. Swaying in ecstasy and singing the song of truth he moved ahead on the difficult path of *Sādhanā*.

## Bibliography

1. 'Researches in Indian History, Archaeology, Art and Religion eds. Kappuram and Kumudamani (Delhi, Sundeep Prakashan, 1990).
2. Bhattacharya, B.D., *The Jaina Iconography* (Delhi, Motilal Banarsidas 1974).
3. उपाध्याय अमर मुनि, महावीर : सिद्धांत और उपदेश (आगरा, सन्मति ज्ञानपीठ, 1986).
4. उपाध्याय अमर मुनि, जैनत्व की झाँकी (आगरा, सन्मति ज्ञानपीठ, 1971).

# Organization of the Narrative in Ākhyānakamaṇikośa

18

*Vimala Bafana*

Nemichandrāchārya is the founder of the composition known as 'Ākhyānakamaṇikośa'. He has four other voluminous compositions also to his credit. Āmradevasūri has elaborated upon the original structure provided by Nemichandrācārya and this is what we know today as 'Akhyānakamaṇikośa vṛtti' (AMKV). Its date of composition is V.S. 1190 (1134 A.D.) and the place Dhavalakkapura, identified with modern Dholka in Gujarat. The book consists of 52 original *gāthās of* Āchārya Nemichandra and *Vṛtti* on these by Āchārya Āmradevasūri, extending to 14000 śloka-measure.

The 12th century A.D. is, no doubt, the golden era of the cultural history of Gujarat. Various kings, like Siddharaja Jayasimhadeva, patronized men of letters and religious teachers of both Jain and non-Jain communities. In this era of literary renaissance Jain monks too were inspired and they produced significant books on various subjects like philosophy, *yoga,* poetry, arts, science, grammar etc. They tried to elevate the moral standards of common people through religious tales and treatises on ethics etc. In these, they advised people, not by dry sermons but by interesting illustrative stories, to lead a religious life for social and individual well-being.

Jain authors preferred to write in Prakrit, Apabhraṁśa or even the contemporary Gujarati. Their works consist of simple easy stories which are full of everyday phrases and idioms. They are simple and appealing. So they could easily reach the common people faster and serve the purpose of their authors. Though simple and lucid they are not lacking in poetic qualities. Figures of speech are used aptly and metres are varied to suit the situation.

Āmradevasūri uses both prose and verse. In respect of language and dialects, he prefers Jain Mahārāṣṭri but switches over to Apabhraṁśa and even Sanskrit wherever such changes promote the narration. The most effective however is his variation of metres, particularly in the Apabhraṁśa portion of the narration.

Reverence towards *deva, guru* and *dharma* is a recurrent theme. Worldly feelings such as those of love, hatred, greed and revenge too are depicted. Thus all the aspects of life are successfully covered.

The original 52 *gāthās* of Nemichandrāchārya constitute the seed of the large tree of this narrative. In the original *gāthās* certain virtues are enunciated and protagonists are cited who practised these and reaped the fruits thereof. The *Vṛtti* elaborates the examples by suitable stories. If we look into the organization of sister narratives such as Kathā-Kośa Prakaraṇa of Jineśwarasūri, Bṛhatkathākośa of Hariṣeṇa and Kathakośa of Śrīchandra, we find the same technique being adopted in these too. Infact, exposition of a virtue or an adage through example story is rooted in the entire gamut of ancient Indian narrative literature. The 6th Agama Nāyādhammakahāo follows this technique. We have nearly the same technique running through the Pañchatantra and Hitopadeśa and even the Jātaka tales to some extent.

In AMKV there are 41 chapters and 126 stories. From the all-times cryptic nature of narration, we may assume that these stories were fairly well-known and often a catch-word was enough for people having some grounding in literature to restore them to memory. This is why Āchārya Nemichandra satisfied himself with just enunciating the virtues and naming their adherents. These key-words must have proved enough for the author and other religious teachers of the time to narrate the corresponding stories in their respective sermons. Nevertheless, it was felt that putting the illustrative stories on record could serve the purpose better, because, then, these could be accessible also to such religious teachers who could not recollect the stories by such scanty promptings. Moreover, once written down they could be read even by the general people without the intervention of a religious teacher. Perhaps with these points in view Āmradevasūri undertook to elaborate upon the hints given by his predecessor Nemichandrāchārya. That the former namely Āmradevasūri, completed the whole work, extending to 14000 śloka-measure, in nine and half months only, should be proof enough that he knew the basic structures of the stories and he had only to give expression to these and spare himself the labours of inventing plots.

These stories are known as 'Nāya' stories (Nāyakahā) which seems to be a derivative of *Jñāta* or *Jñātaka,* so called because of its being well-known in the community. It is also known as 'Dṛṣṭāntakathā'. We may take, from Nāyādhammakahāo, the example of the *tumbaga* (gourd) to illustrate the heaviness and lightness of soul due to accumulation and shedding of Karmas. Wrapped with straw and painted with mud, coat after coat, the *tumbaga* becomes heavier and heavier and when floated on water it sinks. Finally it goes to the bottom. So it is with a soul. Coated with eightfold *Karmas* it sinks to the bottom of *saṁsāra.* Gradually when these coverings *(āvaraṇa)* unfold one by one, the gourd comes up to the surface. It means the moment *Karmas* are washed off from the soul it becomes lighter, pure and real. With above mentioned story one can derive a concrete conclusion that only pure soul can easily reach salvation.

The AMKV is a huge treasure-house of *Nāyas.* Most of these are thought and action oriented. So the fact remains that they are religion-based stories with lot of teaching and inspiration for truth, chastity, self-control, penance and kindness to all the living beings. A constant application to these stories is sure to develop a positive attitude.

Like most moral stories these use birds and animals, besides human beings, as characters. Generally a good number of legendary tales are illustrative of the good or bad results of the practice of virtues and vices. The characters in stories are often known to have attained happiness in this world, or in after life, and even obtained liberation by following the principles preached by the Tīrthaṅkaras.

A very persistent feature of these *dharmakathās* is the motif of *jātismaraṇa,* remembrance of one's previous life, whereby a person obtains solution of some problem of his present life and whereupon he takes to the right path or further consolidates it. Persons' previous lives provide motive to the present ones. This is a specific feature of the Jain narratives. Haribhadrasūri's 'Samarāiccakahā' is a very good example of this technique of plot-construction. In AMKV too, characters are taken to one or more previous lives which explain the conduct of their present life. In story No. 25 a prince Ilāputra, develops an intense love for a low caste forester woman (*mātaṅgī*). He abandons his royalty, becomes a nomad and even stakes his life to win her favour. Later, he discovers that the woman was fickle and didn't deserve that much of devotion. At this stage he has *jātismaraṇa.* He discovers the reason behind his blind lust and then naturally renounces the world and devotes his life to right conduct instead.

On the basis of the above discussion we may summarize the specific features of the organization or story-development of AMKV as follows :

1. The stories grow from the hints provided by Nemichandrāchārya and provide illustration to what has been enunciated by the original author.
2. Characters are often taken to their past life to provide reasons for their present conduct.
3. The sole objective of these stories is religious teaching and it is to this end that the author laboriously directs all his attention.
4. All the stories taken together provide a comprehensive structure of Jain religious conduct.

# Jain Vishva Bharati Institute

**19**

Jain Vishva Bharati Institute (JVBI) has been founded by Gurudeva Tulsi, great seer, saint and scholar of the modern era. His Holiness is the ninth Āchārya, the Supreme Head of the Jain Terāpanth religious sect, comprising more than 700 monks and nuns, and millions of followers all over the country and abroad. Transcending sectarian boundaries, he has been incessantly working during the last six decades for the welfare of mankind–eradicating social evils, reforming social customs, building up national character and educating the masses about the principles of non-violence, universal peace and brotherhood. He has set an unprecedented example of giving up his Āchāryaship during his lifetime, and conferring it on his disciple, Āchārya Mahāprajñya, who is a great thinker, philosopher and writer, often described as a walking encyclopedia of Jainology. These two living legends are the light and the spirit of this organization.

## Motto and Mission

'*Nanassa Saram Ayaro*' 'Character building is the essence of knowledge'. This is the motto of the Institute. Every programme and every activity is directed towards the realisation of this motto.

The mission of the Institute is to integrate modern science with ancient wisdom enshrined in the texts of the great spiritual practitioners and visionary seers of this country. This way, the institution seeks to interweave moral and spiritual norms and values with the materialistic and economic fibres of mankind.

This will foster and develop universal human relationship for the peaceful co-existence of individuals, groups, communities, sects, races, religions and nations. This mission is to be achieved by spreading the Jaina doctrine of 'Anekānt' (non-absolutist and relativistic outlook towards life), practising small vows or 'Anuvrat' (a code of human conduct) and achieving the synthesis of the body, mind and soul through 'Preksha Dhyan' (meditation for the purification of the soul by perceiving one's self).

**Status of the University**

Jain Viśva Bhārati Institute (JVBI) is an autonomous registered society, sponsored and financed by Jain Viśva Bhārati, which is a multiface philanthropic society engaged in the promotion of the values of ancient civilization, particularly in the fields of education, medicine, *sadhanā* (meditation) and research for the last 25 years. In recognition of the vast potential which Jainology offers to humanity as a whole, and to the academic community in particular, as also the valuable services JVB rendered to the society, Government of India, in consultation with University Grants Commission, notified JBVI as "Deemed to be University" under Section 3 of the U.G.C. Act, 1956. By virtue of this statutory status given for the first time to any Jain Institute, JVBI started post-graduate courses from 1992 onwards, and is professionally managed within the broad guidelines of the University Grants Commission. JVBI now plans to become an international centre of studies and research in Jainology, non-violence and peace and value-education.

Dr. Glenn D Paice, Professor Emeritus, Peace Studies Programme, University of Hawaii, in an article published in the International Journal of 'Non-violence' brought out by the American University, Washington D.C. observed :

"The dedication of the new Jain University for non-violence in Lacnun on 26 November, 1992, was surely an historic event that augurs well for the future of non-violent global transformation... the Jain Vishva Bharati Institute justly claimed its new status as deemed university and set forth on a new journey of non-violence, discovery, education and service...it would be quite appropriate for the University to become a global team in developing the theory and practice of non-violence education.

## Relevance of the Institute

There is no dearth of universities and Institutes inside and outside the country. They are fulfilling the aims of education by awarding degrees for getting jobs and preparing the students in the fields of Science, Arts and Commerce. Though this type of university education leads to the advancement of science and technology and sharpens the intellect of students, it increases the tendency of materialistic possession which demands the indiscriminate fulfilment of wants. Consequently, the rules of conduct, the moral values and the ethical content of human lives have received a severe set-back in the current century. The prevalent educational system has inadvertently neglected character building and the attainment of emotional balance, without which human beings, with all their high intellectual knowledge, cannot co-exist peacefully.

The world has now realized that without moral and spiritual education, no amount of material advancement can bring peace in any field of life, whether it is individual or family or community or international relations. Wars are the products of mind. Peace will also have to be found in the mind. Hence, training the mind through the proper teachings of peace is a must for a peaceful world-order.

The problems of the present age are: tension, ecological pollution, violence, cruelty, corruption, drug-addiction, indiscipline, exploitation and inequality. These have arisen due to the degeneration of faith in basic values of life, an utterly materialistic outlook, an excessive proclivity for ease and comfort, unbridled desires and cravings, lack of compassion, excessive greed and selfishness. These subversive tendencies are to be tackled through systematic spiritual education at all levels through the University. The JVBI aspires to fill this gap.

## Location

The Institute is located in Ladnun, a small township of Nagaur District of Rajasthan (India). It is free from pollution and noise, and provides an excellent environment for studies and research. Though surrounded by sand dunes, it has a green and leafy setting, and peaceful atmosphere which can make a person forget the hustle and bustle of cities and tensions of a busy industrial life. Ladnun is 380 Kms. west of Delhi and 225 Km. north west of Jaipur. It is well served by delux and express bus services from Jaipur, Jodhpur, Bikaner, Udaipur, Delhi and other cities. From Delhi, there is an overnight train up to Ratangarh. From Ratangarh, journey to Ladnun is of less than 2 hours duration by road or local train. Nearest airports are Jaipur and Jodhpur. Months of May and June are hot, months of July and August are rainy and months of December, January and February are cold but pleasant. Climate in the remaining months is mild and dry.

## Campus

The campus of Jain Vishva Bharati, sponsoring body of JVBI, is spread over 100600 sq. meters of area with trees on either side of the roads, and parks in the centre. Administrative and Teaching Blocks as well as Boys' hostel are housed in 'Amritayan' an elegant spread-out structure on Sadhana Marg. Women's hostel is in 'Gautam Gyanshala' on Sewabhavi Marg, Jain Vishva Bharati Guest Houses, named 'Satkar', 'Sagar' and 'Sumeru' are on Sadhana Marg. There is a 60-room Meditation Centre, called 'Tulsi Adhyatma Needam' in which meditation camps are held round the year. Library of JVBI, named 'Vardhman Granthagar' has a collection of more than 35,000 books and 5,000 manuscripts. Anekānt Shodhpeeth is the Research Centre, located in Vardhman Granthagar. Besides, there is a centre for teaching computer applications to students and workers of the Institute.

Other facilities in the campus include an English medium primary school (Vimal Vidya Vihar), Ayurvedic health and medical centre (Seva Bhavi Kalyan Kendra), and an Audio-visual centre (Amrit Vani) managed by Jain Vishva Bharati.

Unique feature of the campus is 'Bhikshu Vihar' and 'Prajnalok' in which the Gurudev, the Āchārya, and their disciple monks give regular sermons and provide guidance to the scholars and *Sādhaka* of Jainology. The presence of holy persons (*Sādhus and Sādhvies*) in the campus is so inspiring and blissful that it spontaneously unfolds the inner strength of the body, mind and soul of everyone who come in their contact. There is no discrimination on the basis of caste, creed, sex, nationality and race. Rich and poor are treated alike.

## Academic Programmes

### Post Graduate Courses

Presently, JVBI offers regular, residential, two-year Post Graduate degree courses commencing from July every year in the following disciplines :

### 1. M.A. in Jainology and Comparative Philosophy

Syllabus covers Jain metaphysics, Jain ethics, Jain meditation and Karma theory, mainly based on canonical texts, epistemology, logic and *anekānta*. It also includes comparative study of other schools of Indian Philosophy and Western Philosophy.

### 2. M.Sc. in Science of Living, Preksha Meditation and Yoga

The course is aimed at development of integrated personality through attitudinal change and behavioural modification of the student. Syllabus covers the techniques of stress management, operational efficiency, career development, goal achievement, physical, mental and emotional health, training in non-violence, nervous system, endotrine system, maintenance systems of body, nutrition, ecology and environment, breath and vital energy, value development through meditation (Body, Mind, Psyche), contemplation, auto-suggestion (*Anupreksha),* Indian psychology, psychopathology, psychotherapy, clinical and abonormal psychology etc. (Theory and Practice both).

### 3. M.A. in Non-violence, Peace and Anuvrat

Syllabus covers philosophy of non-violence conflict resolution, methodology of peace research, thought and action of Anuvrat, training in non-violence, peace technology, peace education, environment ethics, ecology etc.

### 4. M.A. in Prakrit Language and Literature

Syllabus covers Ardhamagadhi and Saurasesni canonical texts *(Agam Sahitya)*, history of Prakrit literature, Kāvya literature, grammar, philology, philosophical texts, drama, inspirational prakrit, remnants of Pali and Buddhist hybrid Sanskrit, manuscript editing etc.

The courses offered by the Institute are designed to promote teaching and research in dominant Jain values which are of great relevance in modern society. Unlike other major religions, Jainism does not believe in the authority of God or of any divine book, for it lays utmost importance on man himself who has to search the truth through self-exertion in spiritual practices and to have gimpses of it. It does not believe in any kind of fundamentalism and fanaticism, for its philosophy of *Anekānt* or non-absolutism makes a person view truth from many angles enabling him to practise the synthesis of opposite views, reconciliation, harmony and co-existence.

The doctrine of *Ahiṁsā* or non-violence promotes tolerance towards others, even towards the smallest creature, and promotes forgiveness, fearlessness, forbearance and compassion. The Jain principles of *Aparigraha* or non-possessiveness is of great relevance for environmental preservation and reconstruction of society free from disparity, exploitation and cruelty. The Science of Living, as a new subject, meets the need of value education, moral education, health education and yoga education with its emphasis on scientific study of *Preksha* Meditation. It is a system of self-development and self-management through physiological and psychological techniques.

## Scholarship

Presently, JVBI offers long term scholarship to meritorious and deserving persons desirous of pursuing career in its chosen fields of learning, up to Rs. 10,000 per annum to post graduate students and up to Rs. 18,000 per annum to doctoral scholars. Higher amount is offered to post doctoral research fellows. Four scholarships are reserved for foreign nationals.

## Certificate Course

Certificate course in Science of Living and Preksha Meditation is held during summer months (two months by correspondence and one month by classroom teaching and application) as announced from time to time.

## Correspondence Courses

The Institute has started under-graduate correspondence course under the scheme of Distance Education in the disciplines of Arts, Computer Science, Environmental Science and Ecology and Business Management. These courses are being coordinated from the Institutes Office at Ajmer (Directorate of Distance Education, JVBI, Sunder Bilas Marg, Oppósite Power House, Jaipur Road, Ajmer-305001, Phone No. 423256). For unavoidable reasons, new admissions have been stopped for the time being. Announcement will be made as and when it is resumed.

## Research

JVBI is primarily a research-oriented centre of higher education in Jainology and oriental learning. It lays greater emphasis on research than on teaching and more on quality than on quantity. At present, 32 scholars are pursuing doctoral (Ph. D. research) and two post-doctoral (D. Litt) research on a variety of topics. The research programmes of the institute are being strengthened. In addition to regular students, several scholar monks and nuns are constantly engaged in research on Jaina canonical texts (Āgams) through new interpretations, critical editions, translation and the preparation of critical notes.

## Research Projects Completed

The projects so far completed by JVB and JVBI include critical editing, translation in Hindi with critical annotations and publication of all the main Jain *Agams* containing the messages and principles of omniscient Lord Mahāveera, along with indices and lexicons. The catalogue of these publications can be obtained from the Institute. The complete set costs Rs. 5,800 (discounted price) plus postage charges. The Institute has also published various books authored by members of its faculty. The English translation of *Ayaro* with a new bhaṣya is under publication.

## Proposed Research Projects

1. English Translation of Jain Agams :
   (a) Bhagavati (Viahapannail)

   This is the fifth *aṅga* of the Jain canonical texts. The English translation with critical commentary by Āchārya Mahaprajña has been started by Dr. N.M. Tatia, the Director of Anekānt Shodhapeeṭh with assistance of Muni Shri Mahendra Kumar, the monk Professor of JVBI. The first volume which will contain the first two *shataka* (chapters) is expected to be of 500 pages.

   (b) The English translation of Anuogaddaraim and Nandi is to be taken up shortly.
2. Critical editions and publications of the Niryakhi, Bhāṣyas, Churnis, etc.
3. Interpretation of the doctrine of *anekāntvād* non-absolutism or relativism) in perspective of modern scientific theories.
4. Relevance of the doctrine of non-violence of the Jain philosophy in the perspective of economics, political science, sociology, psychology, ecology and history.

5. Jain Meditation and Yoga (sādhanā), giving a complete historical development from the time of Lord Mahāveera up to *Prekśā Dhyān.*
6. Historical development of Jain thought with their impact on contemporary thought.
7. Jain Astronomy has its peculiar concepts and reveals a very ancient thoery of cosmology. The full-fledged description and the mathematical computation of astrophysical distances would be very fascinating for modern scholars.
8. Prākrit Koś (Cyclopaedic Dictionary)

These projects will be conducted systematically and continuously under the direction of some well known experts already identified. Those interested in offering their services for any of these projects should contact the Institute's authorities.

## Capsule Course for Foreigners

On demand from various scholars of some foreign countries, JVBI has planned a 21-day-capsule-course on 'Doctrines and Application of Jainology, Non-violence, Peace, Science of Living and Prekśā Meditation' during the academic session in 1996. Those desirous of attending the same may write to the Registrar of the Institute so that the detailed programme could be sent to them individually as soon as it is finalised.

## Open to Foreign Scholars and Visitors

The Institute is open to students from abroad for attending regular courses and pursuing regular research (subject to completion of Government formalities). Moreover, those who wish to visit the Institute for short periods for specific study/meditation/non-violence can also be accommodated, if prior intimation is given and the programme is finalised by the Institute in advance. Institute has an access to several guest houses in the campus for making their stay as comfortable as possible within limited resources available in rural India. The members of the faculty as well as the officers of the Institute will spare no means to look after the needs of the visitors. From the point of view of climate, the months from November to March are pleasant and therefore preferable. During this period academic activities of the Institute remain in full swing. Study material on Jain doctrines in English language is under preparation for sending it to those who live abroad and are inquisitive to know the same.

## Extension Programme

The Institute has recently set up a Directorate of Extension activities for undertaking projects of social work. This work is done by cooperation with other sister organizations, namely, Jeevan Vigyan Academy, Preksha Dhyan Academy, Anuvrat Samiti, Anuvibha, schools and colleges sponsored by the same management inside and outside Ladnun. The scope of social work includes eradication of poverty, campaigns against social evils like dowry, obscenity, etc., removal of corruption, prevention of smoking, alcoholism and drug addiction, adult education and non-formal education, serving of physically and mentally handicapped, amelioration of downtrodden and establishment of human rights. Teachers training programmes are organized from time to time.

## Goal

The first and foremost task of this Institute is to develop it as an international centre of Jainology by imparting higher education and preparing scholars in this little explored treasure of knowledge, conducting research in different sciences hidden in Jain Agams and to bring them to light by translating them from Prakrit into Hindi, English and other major languages of the world. This is a challenging job for which the Institute invites every single student and teacher from anywhere interested in Jainology to contact the Vice-chancellor or the Registrar of JVBI.

To make this knowledge useful and relevant to the society, plans are under consideration to start, in due course, integrated value based courses in the professional subjects like Management, Education, Social Work, Computer Science etc. The goal is to produce ideal managers/executives, ideal teachers and ideal social workers with a difference, who will possess a scientific-cum-spiritual personality to work for a non-violent world order. An undergraduate girls college with Honours in Jainology is also proposed to be set up at Ladnun.

# Index